ArtScroll® Series

Rabbi Nosson Scherman / Rabbi Gedaliah Zlotowitz
General Editors

Rabbi Meir Zlotowitz ז״ל, *Founder*

THE Weekly

SEFER SHEMOS ◦ ספר שמות

Rabbi Nachman Zakon

Illustrated by Tova Katz

Published by

ARTSCROLL®
Mesorah Publications, ltd.

The Jaffa Family Edition

Parashah

An illustrated retelling of the Chumash with Midrash

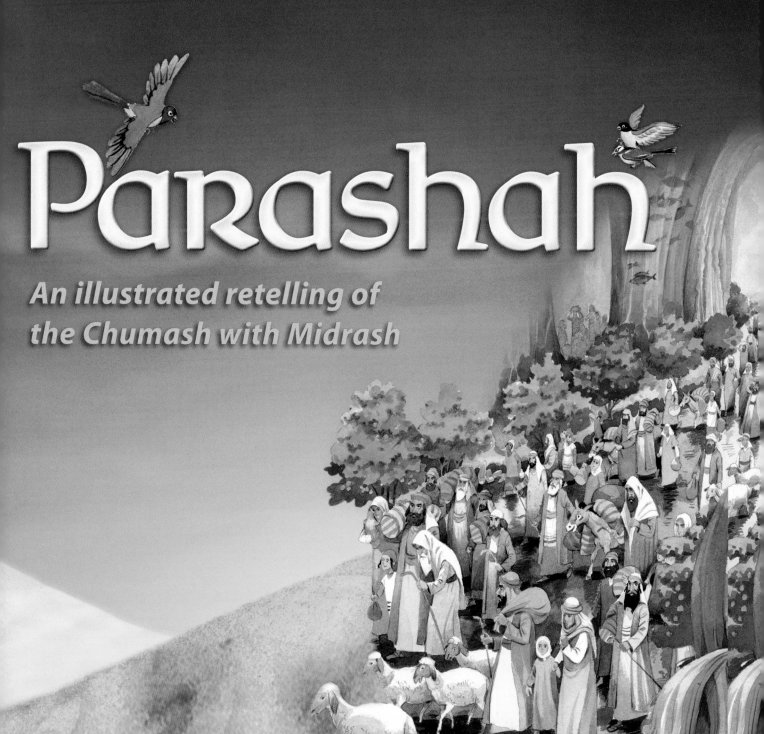

We express special appreciation to
Jacob Schottenstein
for suggesting the concept of this book.
Mature beyond his years, he is already well on
the way to embracing his family legacy.

RTSCROLL® SERIES

"THE WEEKLY PARASHAH — SEFER SHEMOS"

Published by **MESORAH PUBLICATIONS, LTD.**
313 Regina Avenue /Rahway, N.J. 07065 / (718) 921-9000 / Fax: (718) 680-1875
www.artscroll.com

Distributed in Israel by **SIFRIATI / A. GITLER**
POB 2351 / Bnei Brak 5112, Israel

Distributed in Europe by **LEHMANNS**
Unit E, Viking Business Park, Rolling Mill Road / Jarrow, Tyne and Wear / England NE32 3DP

Distributed in Australia and New Zealand by **GOLDS WORLD OF JUDAICA**
3-13 William Street / Balaclava, Melbourne 3183, Victoria, Australia

Distributed in South Africa by **KOLLEL BOOKSHOP**
Northfield Centre / 17 Northfield Avenue / Glenhazel 2192 / Johannesburg, South Africa

Printed in Canada
Custom bound by Sefercraft, Inc. / 313 Regina Avenue /Rahway N.J. 07065
ISBN-10: 1-426-2551-6
ISBN-13: 978-1-4226-2551-4

It is a privilege to dedicate this volume
to our unforgettable friend and mentor

Rabbi Meir Zlotowitz ז״ל
הרב מאיר יעקב בן הגאון הרב אהרן ז״ל

He changed the world and spread Torah study to an unprecedented degree. It is fitting that this *Sefer Shemos* is dedicated to him, because it tells the story of Klal Yisrael receiving the Torah at Har Sinai. Reb Meir was Hashem's agent to bring the Torah to our brothers and sisters everywhere.

He made Torah study accessible to *everyone* — scholar, layman, student, everyone! — and this new work will do the same in a unique and joyous way.

ArtScroll/Mesorah was his vision and he made it his reality. Under the leadership of our beloved friend, Rav Gedaliah, it carries on Rav Meir's dream. With Hashem's help, may he and the rest of the ArtScroll family — *Rav Meir's family* — continue to bring Torah, *yiras Shamayim*, and inspiration to multitudes and generations of our people.

The Jaffa Family

Acknowledgments

My fondest memories of my father are of him telling us the stories of the weekly parashah, with Midrashim. My fascination with the stories of the Torah was born in the glow of the Shabbos candles, lit by my mother. I am gratefully dedicating this project to my parents, Aharon Yosef ben Yochanan HaKohen and Breindel Reizel bas Nachman a"h.

Sefer Shemos focuses on the story of Yetzias Mitzrayim. I dedicate this volume of The Weekly Parashah to my children, Moshe, David and his wife, Tamar, and my grandchildren, Adina, Chananiah, Yosef, and Amichai, with fond memories of the Sedarim that we've shared, and hopes that we will share many more in the future.

My appreciation for Chumash and Midrash grew by leaps and bounds through the inspirational shiurim of my rebbi, Rav Nachman Bulman zt"l.

My writing career has been due to my life's partner, Miriam, who has been an indispensable fountain of help, guidance, and encouragement. This sefer is another product of our partnership.

I must thank my chavrusa, Dr. Pinchas Ackerman, for his unlimited patience throughout the writing of this sefer.

Teaching Torah requires accuracy to ensure that it properly reflects our mesorah, the traditions handed down from generation to generation. Rabbi Pinchas Waldman shlita, my rebbi and mentor, checked the accuracy of this sefer and verified the sources, ensuring the quality and authenticity of the text. I am grateful for all that he has done for our family.

The text went through the expert editorial hands of Rabbi Nosson Scherman and Shmuel Blitz, whose suggestions and edits fine-tuned the original manuscript, putting a polish on it so it sparkles. Rabbi Shlomo Dayan's comments were very valuable; I appreciate his dedication and ability to work under intense deadline pressure.

Thanks to the other members of ArtScroll's professional and caring staff: Rabbi Gedaliah Zlotowitz, for giving me this wonderful opportunity; Rabbi Sheah Brander, for the creative direction that makes every ArtScroll book a masterpiece; Eli Kroen, for his incredible graphic and technical expertise, Mrs. Esther Feierstein, for her meticulous proofreading; Mrs. Rivka Weiss, for providing expert technical assistance; Rabbi Avrohom Biderman, for his input on the illustrations; Mendy Herzberg, for shepherding the many files so efficiently; Rabbi Dovid Morgenstern, for reviewing the work and making important suggestions.

Tova Katz's illustrations have enhanced this work immeasurably, and she was a pleasure to work with. Yonina Hartstein of Divine Design did a beautiful job designing and laying out the book, and creating the extraordinary cover.

After years of telling over the parashah to my young talmidim in a way that would excite and fascinate them, I thank the Almighty that He has given me this opportunity to reach so many more talmidim than I ever could have in the classroom.

Rabbi Nachman Zakon

Table of Contents

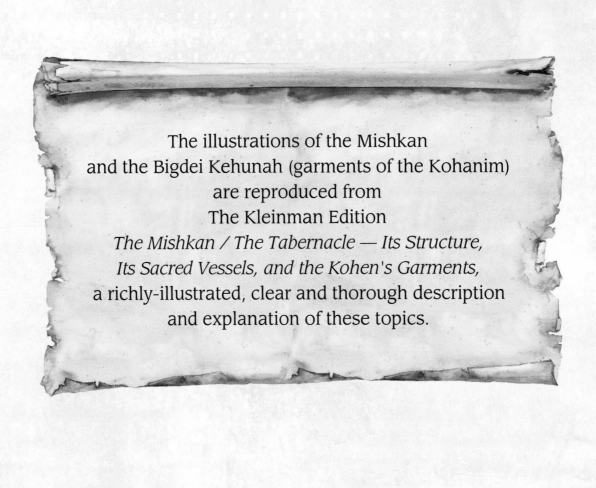

פָּרָשַׁת
שְׁמוֹת

◆

Parashas
Shemos

Shemos · שְׁמוֹת

Parashah Pointers

‣ Yosef dies and Egypt gets a new king.

‣ The Jewish population grows miraculously.

‣ Pharaoh says all baby boys should be killed.

‣ The Jews become slaves in Egypt.

‣ Moshe is born and adopted by the princess of Egypt.

‣ Moshe kills an Egyptian who was beating a Jew.

‣ Moshe stops a fight between two Jews.

‣ Moshe escapes from Egypt and goes to Midian.

‣ Moshe marries Tziporah.

‣ Moshe's children are born.

‣ Hashem speaks to Moshe from a burning bush.

‣ Hashem appoints Moshe to take the Jews out of Egypt.

‣ Moshe and Aharon tell Pharaoh to free the Jews.

‣ Pharaoh is angry and forces the Jews to work even harder.

‣ The Jews blame Moshe for making their life even worse.

‣ Moshe complains to Hashem.

Good Times

aakov, his sons, and their families had moved to Egypt. Life seemed wonderful there. They were very well off. Egypt was the most important country in the world. Their brother Yosef was the second most powerful man in Egypt, and he took care of the family.

The older generation passed away. First Yaakov died. One by one, Yaakov's sons, the shevatim, passed away. Yosef was the first to die and Levi was the last.

As long as any of the shevatim were alive, life was good for the Jews in Egypt. This lasted almost a hundred years.

Then the troubles started.

Living so comfortably in Egypt, the Jews started behaving like the Egyptians. Some of them even served idols.

But there were four things they did to remain Jewish:

1. They used Jewish names.
2. They did not speak lashon hara.
3. They behaved modestly.
4. They spoke Hebrew, the holy language.

Hashem's Promise

Hashem had told Avraham Avinu that his children would suffer in exile, and then, later, He would take them to Eretz Yisrael. It was now time for the suffering to start.

Tricked!

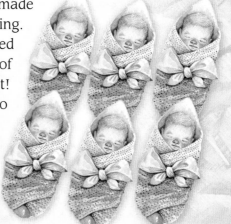n Egypt the Jews were blessed with large families — VERY large families. Women gave birth to SIX babies at a time! That bothered the Egyptians. There were just so many Jews everywhere!

The ruler of Egypt by this time was a new Pharaoh. He made believe he never heard that Yosef had saved Egypt from starving. Pharaoh was worried that his country was in danger. He believed that if Egypt was attacked, all the Jews would fight on the side of the enemy. They might even throw the Egyptians out of Egypt! Pharaoh called his three advisers — Bilaam, Iyov, and Yisro — to discuss what to do.

"Destroy them!" Bilaam said firmly.

Iyov kept quiet.

"Leave the Jews alone," Yisro protested.

The wicked Pharaoh decided to listen to Bilaam. He would

destroy the Jews! He would turn them into slaves, forcing them to work harder and harder.

Pharaoh tricked the Jews into becoming slaves. He announced a new building project in the cities of Pisom and Ramses. He asked all good citizens to come, to make bricks and help build the new cities. Even Pharaoh himself showed up carrying a basket and a shovel. He tried to show everyone how important the work was. He even worked together with the others.

The Jews came too. They worked along with everyone else, making bricks and putting up new buildings. They worked extra hard that day, harder than anyone else. They were good workers, eager to show how much they could do. At the end of the day, Pharaoh's men wrote down how many bricks each Jew had made.

The next time the Jews arrived at Pisom and Ramses, they got the shock of their lives. They were the only ones there! No Egyptians had come to work. Pharaoh's soldiers surrounded them. "By Pharaoh's orders you are now slaves to Egypt," they declared. "You will spend your days making bricks." The Jews asked, "How many?" "The same number of bricks that you made on that first day."

Only one group of Jews didn't become slaves. That was Shevet Levi. They had ignored Pharaoh's first call for workers to build his cities. Their reason? They weren't going to stop their holy work of Torah study to go and make bricks. The Torah hadn't been given yet, but they learned about how to serve Hashem the way Avraham, Yitzchak, and Yaakov had served Him.

Failure!

Pharaoh wanted to make sure the Jews did not have many children, so he made the slave laborers work very hard. But Hashem had different plans: The harder Pharaoh would make them work, the more Jewish babies would be born!

Pharaoh saw that his plan wasn't working. There were more Jews than when he started making them slaves! It must be that they weren't working hard enough, he thought, so he gave them even more work to do. When they came home at night, they were forced to serve the Egyptians, cleaning their homes, cooking and baking for them until late into the night. They had to clean the streets. They planted and harvested in the fields. The Egyptians even forced them to risk their lives capturing wild animals for them.

The Egyptian supervisors beat the Jews. They suffered terribly. Slavery was awful. But soon things were going to get even worse...

The Dream

One night Pharaoh had a terrifying dream.

He was sitting on his throne when an old man suddenly appeared. The man took all the princes and leaders of Egypt and put them on a scale. Then he took a little lamb and put it on the other side of the scale. The lamb weighed more than all of Pharaoh's men!

"How could one small lamb be heavier than all his government ministers?" Pharaoh wondered.

After Pharaoh woke up, he called an emergency meeting of all the wise men who knew how to find the meaning in dreams. After Pharaoh told them about his nightmare, they were scared. "The dream means that a Jewish boy will be born," one of them said. "He will destroy all of Egypt."

Pharaoh was determined to save himself and his country. If this boy would destroy Egypt, he would make sure the boy would not live.

The decision was made: They would kill all the Jewish baby boys. But how? Even though the Egyptians worshiped idols, they knew that the Jewish G-d was powerful. What if Hashem would take revenge against those who killed His people?

They tried to think of ways to outsmart Hashem. One Egyptian came up with an idea. He remembered that Hashem had promised Noach that He would never again bring a flood. If they ordered all Jewish boys thrown into the Nile River to drown, Hashem couldn't punish the Egyptians using water!

This Egyptian was right, and he was also really wrong. Yes, Hashem would not flood the entire world, but He could still flood one country. At the end, instead of bringing water to Egypt, Hashem brought the Egyptians to the water, when He drowned them during the great miracle of Kriyas Yam Suf (the Splitting of the Sea).

Soon the new law was announced throughout the land: All Egyptians were to look for Jewish baby boys — and throw them into the Nile!

The Divorce

The Jews heard the awful news: their newborn sons were doomed to death!

Amram, a grandson of Levi, was the leader of the Jews. When he heard about the new law, he thought, "Why should we have children if they are going to be killed?" With great sadness, he divorced his wife, Yocheved. Many Jews followed Amram's example and got divorced.

Then Miriam, Amram's daughter, told her father something that made him change his mind. "Pharaoh's evil order was only against the boys," she said, "but if you are not married, there won't be any girls either!"

Because of Miriam's words, Amram made a public wedding celebration and remarried Yocheved. Their children, Aharon and Miriam, danced joyously at their parents' new wedding. All the Jews got married again.

Miriam had brought new hope to the Jews!

FASCINATING FACTS

Amram was such a tzaddik that he never sinned in his whole life!

Yocheved

▶ Her father was Levi, the son of Yaakov.

▶ When Yaakov's family went down to Egypt, Yocheved was born just as her mother entered the country.

▶ She was the mother of Aharon, Moshe, and Miriam.

▶ She gave birth to Moshe when she was 130 years old!

FASCINATING
FACTS

The day Moshe was put in the river was the sixth of Sivan, which would be the day the Torah would be given at Har Sinai.

When Noach made his teivah, it was covered on the outside and inside with tar to keep it waterproof. Here, the outside of Moshe's basket was protected with tar, but the inside was coated with clay. This way, the great tzaddik Moshe did not have to smell the unpleasant odor of tar.

Murder!

Shifrah and Puah were nurses who helped Jewish women give birth. (Their real names were Yocheved, who was Moshe's mother, and Miriam, who was his sister.) One sad day Pharaoh called them in and ordered them to kill all the Jewish baby boys as soon as they were born. He didn't mind keeping the girls alive. He figured the Egyptians would marry them when they got older.

These courageous and holy women did no such thing! A few months later Pharaoh realized they weren't following his orders. He brought them back to the palace. He was very angry and asked them why they didn't obey him. They answered wisely that Jewish women didn't call for a nurse until after the baby was already born. By a miracle Pharaoh accepted their excuse and did not punish them!

Food From Rocks

Once again Jewish children were being born. The question was how to make sure that the Egyptians didn't drown the newborn baby boys.

The Jewish mothers decided to have their babies in the forests, so the soldiers wouldn't find them. They would leave them in the forest. The mothers were sure that Hashem would take care of their children.

They were right! Hashem sent each baby two rocks. When the baby was hungry he would suck on the rocks. From one rock the baby drank honey. From the other rock, the baby drank oil. The babies grew big and strong on their Heaven-sent food. When they were old enough, they left the forest and went back to their homes. A miracle happened. Hashem let the children know exactly where their parents lived. Imagine their parents' joy when their children walked in the door and the families were together again.

And the Egyptians never figured out where all the new Jews were coming from!

Baby Moshe

After Amram and Yocheved remarried, Yocheved gave birth to a beautiful baby boy. The whole house was filled with a heavenly light when he was born. She named him Tov, which means good.

Afraid the Egyptians would find him, Yocheved put her baby into a waterproof basket. She put the basket in the Nile River, where it floated on the water. She left her daughter, Miriam, to see what would happen. Miriam stood close enough to keep an eye on her baby brother.

Miriam noticed Pharaoh's daughter, Princess Bisya, walking to the river. Bisya had a skin disease called tzaraas. Bathing in the river's cool

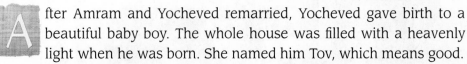

waters made her skin feel better.

Bisya saw the basket. Why was a waterproof basket floating on the river?

She stretched out her hand toward the basket — but she couldn't reach it! She stretched as hard as she could, trying to grab the basket before the river would sweep the baby away! Suddenly, a miracle happened. Her hand *strrrrreeeeetched* out far enough to grab the basket!

And then another miracle! When Bisya touched the basket, her skin disease disappeared!

The princess looked into the basket and saw a baby crying. She said that this must be a Jewish baby. She pitied him and decided to take care of him as if he were her own son. She named him "Moshe" because she pulled him out of the water. (The word "mashah" means to pull out.) It was the perfect name for the baby, who would grow up to "pull out" the Jews from Egypt!

From her hiding place in the bushes, Miriam saw what had happened. Bisya gave Moshe to several Egyptian nursemaids to feed him, but he would not nurse from them. Miriam then ran over to Bisya and asked if she should get a Jewish woman to nurse the baby. Bisya agreed, and Miriam ran home and brought Yocheved, Moshe's mother. Bisya gave her

WHO'S WHO IN THE TORAH

Bisya

▸ She was Pharaoh's daughter, who saved Moshe and adopted him.

▸ She converted and became a Jew on the day she found Moshe.

▸ She left Egypt with all of the Jews.

the baby and even paid her to nurse and care for him. For two years Moshe was raised by his own mother in a Jewish home.

The Palace

When Moshe was two he moved into the palace with the princess, who loved him like a mother. Often she would bring him to Pharaoh, who would put Moshe on his lap and play with him.

On one of these visits Pharaoh was meeting with his advisers while holding Moshe on his lap. All of a sudden Moshe reached up and took Pharaoh's golden crown. Then he put it — on his own head! Seeing this, Pharaoh's advisers became upset. They thought it was a bad sign. "Maybe this is the baby who will take Egypt away from you and make himself king," they told Pharaoh. "The child is dangerous. Kill him!"

The Test

Fortunately for Moshe there was one adviser, Yisro, who told the king, "Why is everyone getting so upset? He's only two years old. He didn't know what he was doing. Young children always grab shiny things. Let's test him. We'll put gold and a glowing coal in front of him. Let's see which one he grabs."

So they put a piece of gold and a red-hot piece of coal in front of Moshe. The advisers and Pharaoh waited to see what Moshe would reach for. Would he reach for the glowing coal, proof that he was just playing when he took the king's crown? Or would he reach for the gold — and death?

Moshe raised his hand to reach for — the gold! Just in time, though, something pushed his hand away, and he grabbed the glowing coal instead. Moshe had passed the test. He would live! But — Ouch! The coal was hot! Instead of dropping it, he put it in his mouth and burnt his tongue. From then on Moshe couldn't speak clearly.

What pushed Moshe's hand? It was the angel Gavriel. Hashem sent him to make sure Moshe passed the test and was not put to death.

Shabbos Rest

When Moshe's mother was nursing him, she had taught him that he was Jewish. Though Moshe lived in the palace like a prince, he cared about his Jewish brothers who were suffering every day. He felt so bad that he cried for them. When he could, he tried to help them. He had an idea.

The Egyptians made the Jews work seven days a week. Moshe had a plan to give them a day of rest. He couldn't just tell Pharaoh, "Give the Jews one day off because I can't stand seeing how badly you treat them."

FASCINATING FACTS

Bisya's reward for her kindness in saving the baby was that the name she gave him — "Moshe" — is the one we call him by.

Pharaoh hated the Jews; he would never listen.

Instead, Moshe told Pharaoh, "If you keep working the Jews every day, they will die. You won't have any slaves left to work for you."

By now Pharaoh liked having all these slaves. He didn't like the idea of losing them, so he told Moshe to give the Jews a day off. Yocheved had taught Moshe about Shabbos, so Moshe ordered that from now on every seventh day — Shabbos — the Jews would not have to work. You can imagine how happy the Jews were to hear that!

Moshe had helped his people — and Pharaoh didn't have a clue that he'd been outsmarted!

Moshe Saves a Jew

When Moshe was 20 years old something happened that would change his life. His comfortable life in the palace would be over.

Moshe saw an Egyptian guard hitting a Jewish slave. The Egyptian was whipping him so hard that the Jew would die.

Moshe looked in every direction. No one was around. He carefully said the holiest Name of Hashem, and the Egyptian instantly fell down dead!

Killing an Egyptian guard was a huge crime in Egypt, punishable by death. Moshe knew that if he were discovered, he'd be in big trouble, so he buried the Egyptian in the sand.

The next day, when Moshe went out for a walk, he saw two Jews arguing. This was so hard for him to understand. With all the problems the Jews had with the Egyptians, you would think they would never fight with each other. But these were two wicked men, Dassan and Aviram.

They were so angry at each other that Dassan actually picked up his fist to hit Aviram.

Moshe had seen enough. He said to Dassan, "Rasha, wicked person! Why would you want to hit another Jew?"

Dassan was angry that Moshe was stopping him. He shouted, "Who are you to tell us what to do? Are you going to kill me like you killed the Egyptian guard?"

When Moshe heard that, he was very frightened. His secret was out. He would be caught and killed.

Dassan and Aviram were so angry at Moshe that they told Pharaoh that he had killed the guard!

Escape

Pharaoh was furious that Moshe had killed an Egyptian. He ordered Moshe captured and publicly beheaded by a sword.

Moshe was brought before Pharaoh. Many others came to watch. Pharaoh's guard lifted his sharp sword and brought it down on Moshe's neck.

Nothing happened. Moshe's neck had turned to marble! The sword had no effect on Moshe's neck! It just bounced off his neck!

Then something even stranger happened. Some of Pharaoh's men suddenly became blind. Others became deaf. And Pharaoh couldn't give any orders — because he couldn't speak!

Now was the time to escape. Moshe ran away from Egypt, leaving everything he knew.

Moshe Protects the Weak

Exhausted from his travels, Moshe stopped at a well in Midian to take a drink of water and rest a little. As he sat there, seven shepherdesses came by with their sheep. They were sisters, the daughters of Yisro. He had been Pharaoh's adviser, who'd tried to save the Jews. He had once also been the high priest of Midian's idols, a very important man. That is, until the day he looked around at the statues that couldn't talk or move and said, "This is all nonsense!"

Yisro told the Midianites that he didn't believe in idols anymore. The Midianites did not like that at all. They decided not to have anything to do with him. No one would work for him or talk to him. With no choice, his seven daughters had to take care of the family's sheep.

TORAH IN OUR LIVES

Even though Moshe was seconds away from death, he never gave up hope that Hashem would save him.

No matter how sick or hurt someone is, don't give up hope and keep praying because Hashem can save him. And no matter how bad things seem to be for you, you should still believe that Hashem can make things better in just one second. He can do anything — even turn a neck into marble.

Moshe watched Yisro's daughters begin the hard job of drawing heavy buckets of water up from the well. They then poured the water into a large, hollowed-out stone for the animals to drink from.

While their animals were drinking, some shepherds came by. They were mean. They pushed Yisro's daughters into the water, then they brought their own sheep to drink the water Yisro's daughters had pulled out of the well.

Moshe saw the girls being treated badly by the other shepherds. Moshe chased the shepherds away.

When the evil shepherds were gone, Moshe told the seven girls to rest. He would pull up water for their sheep. Moshe drew more water for the sheep to drink.

Moshe Gets a New Job

Yisro's daughters went home and told their father, "You will not believe what happened to us today. We were attacked by shepherds at the well and a stranger rescued us!"

"So why did you leave him there?" Yisro answered. "Go and bring the man who saved you."

Yisro's oldest daughter, Tziporah, immediately hurried and brought Moshe to their home. When Yisro found out that Moshe had no place to stay, he invited him to move in with them. Moshe found a new home and became a shepherd, taking care of Yisro's sheep.

A Stick and a Match

Sticking out of the ground in Yisro's garden was an amazing walking stick. It was beautiful, made of blue sapphire stone. The stick was very, very special and very, very old, and had great powers. Hashem had given it to Adam, the first man.

How did the stick wind up stuck in the ground of Yisro's backyard?

For thousands of years the stick was passed from tzaddik to tzaddik. Before Adam died, he gave the stick to Chanoch.

Chanoch gave it to Shem.

Shem gave it to Avraham.

Avraham gave it to Yitzchak.

Yitzchak gave it to Yaakov.

Yaakov gave it to Yosef.

When Yosef died, the stick remained in Pharaoh's palace. When Yisro left Egypt he took it with him.

QUESTIONS, ANYONE?

The Torah tells us only three stories about the first eighty years of Moshe's life — how he killed the brutal Egyptian guard, stopped one Jew from hitting another Jew, and saved the shepherd girls who were being bullied. Why only these three?

The Torah wants to show us what was so special about Moshe, and why Hashem chose him to take the Jews out of Egypt. Moshe couldn't bear to see other people get hurt. He jumped in and helped them right away. That's the kind of leader Hashem wanted for the Jews — someone who would care for them and protect them!

When Yisro arrived in Midian, he put the stick into the ground. Later, when he tried to go near it to pull it out, he wasn't able to. Many strong people tried to go as well, but they had no luck! They couldn't come close!

Finally, Yisro offered a reward: Anyone who could remove the stick would be allowed to marry his daughter Tziporah.

When Moshe saw the stick, he noticed that it had Hebrew writing on it. Curious, he reached over and pulled it out. It came out easily, with no effort at all! The stick had been waiting for Moshe to come and get it.

This wondrous stick would be the one that Moshe would use when Hashem would make many of the miracles in Egypt and in the desert.

On the stick were written the letters באחב עדש דצך. These ten letters represented the Makkos, the Ten Plagues that Hashem would bring against the Egyptians. Together, the letters spelled "d'tzach adash b'achav" — words that we say every year at the Pesach Seder!

When Yisro saw Moshe walk in with the stick, he was amazed. He realized Moshe was someone very special, and he gave him the reward he'd promised. Moshe married Tziporah.

After their marriage the new couple was blessed with their first child. Moshe named him Gershom, which means "a stranger there," because Moshe was a stranger in a foreign land.

A Burning Bush

oshe didn't want the sheep to graze in other people's land. That would be stealing. Instead, he took them out into the desert. Since that land didn't belong to anyone, the sheep could eat all they wanted.

One day, he took his flock to a faraway mountain. The mountain's name was Har Sinai! Though Moshe didn't know it, this was the holy place where one day he would bring the Torah to the Jews.

But that would be in the future. Now, Moshe saw the strangest thing: a sneh, thornbush, that was on fire, but it wasn't burning up!

Strange. Very strange. This was the desert, which is very hot and dry. The plants that grow in the desert catch fire very, very quickly. And yet, though the bush was on fire, its branches and leaves weren't turning black or burning into ashes. They weren't burning up at all!

Why Choose Moshe?

ashem wanted Moshe to pay attention to the bush that didn't burn. It was time for Hashem to send Moshe on his mission: to take the Jews out of Egypt.

Why was Moshe the one Hashem chose?

Moshe was a tzaddik. He was good to others and he loved Hashem. He was already eighty years old. Though he had left Egypt many years before, Moshe still thought about the suffering of his people, the Jews, all the time. He never forgot them.

This was the kind of person Hashem chose to be the leader who would take care of His people — a tzaddik who loved the Jews so much, that many years later he was still thinking about them.

Message of the Thornbush

he thornbush was a lot like the Jews. A thorny little bush seems to be the least important of the trees. It is much less important than beautiful maple trees or tall oaks. In the same way, at that time the Jews seemed to be the least important nation in the world. But just as the bush wasn't destroyed by fire, the Jews also will never be destroyed, no matter how hard our wicked enemies try. This was Hashem's message to Moshe. And it's also Hashem's message to us!

Moshe, Moshe

s Moshe was looking at the burning bush, Hashem called out to him, "Moshe! Moshe!"

Hashem told Moshe to remove his shoes because the place he was standing on was holy ground. It was holy because Hashem was there. Moshe realized that Hashem was talking to him. He was terrified. He covered his face out of fear and respect for Hashem.

GO!

ashem told Moshe, "I am the G-d of Avraham, Yitzchak, and Yaakov. It is time to save the Jews from Egypt and bring them to Eretz Yisrael, a land flowing with milk and honey. Go! I am sending you to Pharaoh to take the Jews out of Egypt."

Not Going

oshe was very humble. He didn't think he was great enough to do such a big job. For seven days Moshe tried to prove to Hashem that He shouldn't send him.

He told Hashem, "How can I be Your messenger? I am a nobody, not important at all; why would Pharaoh listen to me?"

Another argument: "How will I feed so many people when we leave Egypt?"

Hashem told Moshe not to worry. He would be with him and take care of everything. Hashem promised Moshe that he would be successful and that he would bring the Jews to this very mountain to receive the Torah.

Moshe asked, "When I tell this to the Jews, they are going to ask me, 'What is Hashem's Name?' What should I tell them?"

Hashem answered, "Tell them E-heyeh Asher E-heyeh, which means 'I Shall Be As I Shall Be,' sent you." Hashem has many Names, which show different ways that He cares for us. The Name "I Shall Be As I Shall Be" tells us: "I have not forgotten you, I shall always be with you in your troubles in Egypt or anywhere else. And I will save you."

Hashem continued to speak with Moshe. "Go and gather all the Jewish wise men. Tell them these words: 'pakod pakadeti, remember, I have remembered' — to take you out of Egypt and bring you all to Eretz Yisrael."

Hashem told Moshe to use the words "pakod pakadeti" for a very special reason. These two words were code words. Many years before, Yosef told his brothers that these words would be used by the person whom Hashem would send to save the Jews.

"You and the Jewish wise men should go to Pharaoh's palace," Hashem commanded. "Tell Pharaoh that he should let the Jewish people go for a three-day trip to serve Hashem. He won't let them go, so I will punish him with great miracles. Afterward Pharaoh will finally send you away from Egypt. When the Jews leave they will be wealthy, carrying Egypt's silver and gold with them."

"The Jews won't believe me," Moshe objected. "They will say I made the whole thing up, that You never spoke to me."

Moshe should never have said that the Jews wouldn't believe him. It was lashon hara on the Jews. He should have realized that the Jews have faith in Hashem and in His messengers.

Snakes, Tzaraas, and Water

Hashem gave Moshe three signs to prove to the Jews that Hashem sent him. First, Hashem told Moshe to throw his stick on the ground. (Yes, that was the stick from Yisro's garden!) Moshe did it and the stick turned into a snake! Hashem told Moshe to pick it up and it turned back into a stick.

For the next sign, Hashem told Moshe to put his hand inside his robe and take it out again. When Moshe's hand came out it was covered with tzaraas. Moshe put his hand back inside his robe and his hand came out instantly healed. No whiteness at all, just healthy skin.

The final sign was that Moshe should take water from the Nile River and spill it on the ground. When it hit the ground the water would turn into blood.

Hashem used the sign of the snake and tzaraas to give a hint to Moshe. By speaking badly about the Jews — saying they would not believe him — he was behaving like the snake in Gan Eden, the Garden of Eden, who spoke badly about Hashem to Chavah. Tzaraas

Why did Hashem use the two words "pakod pakadeti," which mean almost the same thing — "remember, I remember" — as the code words? One word — "pakadeti, I remember" — should have been enough.

The Jews needed Hashem to save them in two ways. One was to save them from the brutal slavery that made them weak and broken. And the second was to make them a holy people, the way they used to be when Yaakov was still alive. They had lived with the Egyptians for so long, they started acting like them. Hashem would have to lift them up from the low spiritual level of Egypt.

is a punishment for speaking lashon hara, and that's why it appeared on Moshe's hand.

Finally, the third sign was a message to the Jews, telling them that the first makkah (plague) Hashem would punish the Egyptians with would be the makkah that turned all the water into blood.

Angry!

Even after the signs and everything Hashem said, Moshe wouldn't give up. Again, he said he wasn't the right man for the job. "I can't speak properly," he said. (Moshe had burnt his tongue with a hot coal when he was a little boy, so he didn't speak clearly.)

That argument didn't work: Hashem told him that He would give him the power to speak properly.

Even though Moshe was humble, he should have understood that it was time to do what Hashem wanted.

But Moshe didn't stop.

"Send someone else!" he said. He meant that Hashem should send an angel, just like He had done to save Lot from S'dom's destruction.

Why was Moshe so against going? Didn't he want to help the Jews?

The reason was that Moshe loved his older brother, Aharon, very much. Aharon had been the leader of the Jews in Egypt for many years. How would Aharon feel if his younger brother came and took over? Moshe didn't want to make his brother feel bad.

Now Hashem got angry. For seven days He had told Moshe to go, and for seven days Moshe argued that he was not the right person to send. Even though Hashem had answered all his objections, Moshe kept saying no.

"Because of what you have done," Hashem said, "Aharon will be the Kohen and not you. You won't have to worry about how you speak. Aharon will go with you. You tell him what to say and he will speak for you."

Hashem also told Moshe that Aharon would not be upset. Not only that, Aharon would be happy that his younger brother had been picked to take the Jews out of Egypt.

Finally, Moshe agreed to lead the Jews out of Egypt.

The time had come!

FASCINATING FACTS

The donkey that Moshe and his family were riding was no regular donkey. It was very, very old. And it is still alive today!

This was the same donkey that Avraham took with him when he was bringing Yitzchak as a korban at Akeidas Yitzchak.

And who will be riding this donkey once again? Mashiach, when he comes to end our long, long exile!

Back to Egypt

oshe raced home. Every minute counted. The quicker he got to Egypt, the faster the Jews would be free! He packed up his belongings and asked permission from his father-in-law, Yisro.

Moshe and his family got ready to leave. But Moshe had a problem. His newborn son, Eliezer, hadn't had his bris milah yet! But if he gave him a bris, it would be dangerous for him to travel. Moshe would have to wait until the bris healed.

Though it's important to have a bris on time, there was no time to lose. Every day the Jews were suffering more and more!

What should Moshe do?

He decided it was more important to obey Hashem and get to Egypt right away.

Moshe put his wife and children on a donkey, and the family began the long trip to Egypt. They were off to save the Jews!

Tziporah Saves Moshe's Life

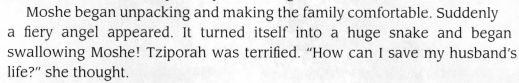

fter traveling the whole day, Moshe and his family passed an inn. It seemed to be the perfect place to rest from their trip and spend the night.

Moshe began unpacking and making the family comfortable. Suddenly a fiery angel appeared. It turned itself into a huge snake and began swallowing Moshe! Tziporah was terrified. "How can I save my husband's life?" she thought.

"The baby! He needs a bris!" Quickly, Tziporah took Eliezer and gave him a bris. As soon as it was done, the angel/snake disappeared. Tziporah's quick thinking had saved Moshe's life.

What did Moshe do that he deserved such a scary fate? He was right to delay the bris because he had to go free the Jews. But once he stopped traveling he should have given his son a bris right away, before unpacking and moving into the inn.

The Brothers Meet

hile this was going on, Hashem spoke to Aharon, in Egypt, and told him to go to Har Sinai. There he would meet his brother.

Aharon reached the mountain just as Moshe and his family got there. When they saw each other, Aharon hugged and kissed Moshe, overjoyed and so excited to meet him for the first time in many, many years!

Moshe introduced his wife and children to his brother. Aharon asked Moshe, "Why are you bringing them to Egypt? There are already so many Jews suffering in Egypt. Why bring more?"

Moshe, of course, listened to his older brother and sent his family back to Midian.

Then Moshe and Aharon traveled together to Egypt.

Wonderful News

When they arrived, Aharon told the Jews the happy news. Freedom was coming! Hashem had sent Moshe to take them out of Egypt, and Aharon was to be his spokesman. Aharon said the code words "pakod pakadeti," and then showed them the signs. The Jews watched as Moshe's walking stick turned into a snake, his hand got tzaraas and immediately recovered, and the river water turned into blood.

When they heard Aharon say the code words of freedom, the Jews knew Hashem had sent Moshe and Aharon!

What did they do when they heard the great news? They bowed down and thanked Hashem for His promise to end their suffering.

On the Way to Pharaoh's Palace

And now it was time. Moshe, Aharon, and the Jewish sages were going to confront the most powerful man in the world. They were going to demand that Pharaoh listen to Hashem and let his slaves leave the country.

A strange thing happened on their way to the palace. One by one, the wise men turned back. They were afraid of Pharaoh, and of what he would do to them when they asked him to free the Jewish people. First there were seventy men … then sixty men … fifty … And by the time Moshe and Aharon got to the huge palace gates they were on their own. Just the two of them.

Getting In

The palace gates were locked and guarded by tough Egyptian soldiers. How were they going to get in? Suddenly, Hashem sent the angel Gavriel to miraculously bring them into the palace.

But being in the palace didn't mean they could see Pharaoh. They still had to get into his throne room. You couldn't just knock on the door and walk in. It was guarded by wild animals like ferocious lions and other beasts. The animals attacked anyone trying to get in without permission.

The lions roared at the two Jews who stood before them, ready to attack! Moshe waved his sapphire stick over the animals — and instead of attacking them, the animals walked over to them, wagging their tails in friendship! The lions were as friendly as little puppies. The tigers were as tame as pussycats!

Escorted by the friendly animals, Moshe and Aharon walked into Pharaoh's throne room.

What would await them there?

Happy Birthday!

The room was full of noise and people. There was a big celebration going on. It was Pharaoh's birthday party! Besides important Egyptians, there were kings from many other countries. Everyone had come to celebrate Pharaoh's birthday.

What do people bring to birthday parties? Presents, of course! There were lines of guests with expensive gifts of crowns for Pharaoh. Each one waited for his turn to wish Pharaoh a happy birthday.

The last to enter the room were Moshe and Aharon. The noise stopped. The room grew very quiet. All eyes were on the two holy tzaddikim.

With the fearsome and friendly beasts still behind them, Moshe and Aharon walked up to Pharaoh's throne.

Pharaoh Refuses

Moshe and Aharon stared at the man sitting before them. Though he was so powerful, Pharaoh was actually very short. He had a long beard, and wore a crown on his head.

Looking at the two Jews, Pharaoh, mighty Pharaoh, grew terrified. In a low, trembling voice, he managed to squeak out, "What do you want?"

"The G-d of the Jews has sent us," they answered, "to tell you to send His people out so they can serve Him in the desert."

Pharaoh got angry! No one *ever* told him what to do. He was Pharaoh, king of Egypt!

"Who is this G-d?" he said sharply. "I never heard of him." Pharaoh went into a room in his palace and picked up a large book that listed all the idols of Egypt and other countries. Pharaoh looked through it, looked up at Moshe and Aharon with a smirk on his face, and said, "Your G-d is not here."

He may have been the "birthday boy," and the most powerful leader in the world, but Pharaoh was also foolish. Did he really expect to find the Name of our living G-d in a book of dead stone and golden idols?

"Tell me," asked Pharaoh, "is your god a young, mighty warrior? What does He do?"

"He created the world, everything in it, and He gives you life."

Now Pharaoh wasn't frightened. He was just plain angry! "Liars! I am the master of the world. I created myself and the Nile River. I will not send out the Jews."

Moshe and Aharon repeated their request. "Let us go for a three-day trip into the desert to worship G-d."

"You want me to lose the work of hundreds of thousands of slaves for three days?" Pharaoh answered. "It's impossible!" He glared at them. "This is not your business! Don't try to stop my slaves from working."

Moshe and Aharon realized it was a waste of time to continue talking to Pharaoh. They turned around and left the palace.

Work Harder!

Pharaoh was burning mad at Moshe and Aharon. What chutzpah! Telling him to give his slaves a vacation!

He called the officers who were in charge of the slaves. "The problem with the Jews is that they are lazy," he said. "They don't want to work. That's why they are asking to leave."

His voice was hard and cold. "From now on, no more days off. We make life too easy for them. Instead of giving them the straw they need to make bricks, they will have to go out and gather straw on their own. Force them to make as many bricks as they did when we gave them straw. That will keep them busy and stop them from asking for days off!"

When they heard the awful news, the Jews were crushed. They were sure they were going to be free. Instead, their troubles got worse! They were forced to work more and were beaten harder than before Moshe had come to them.

Where was Moshe? they wondered. No one could find him.

They didn't know that after his meeting with Pharaoh, Moshe went back to Midian.

Six Months Later

Six difficult months passed. The Jews couldn't take it anymore. The extra work was unbearably hard. Worse, wherever they went to pick straw, Egyptians would bully them, pick on them, and beat them. There was no one to protect them.

The Jewish foremen, who were in charge of making sure the work went smoothly, finally went to Pharaoh. They begged and pleaded with him to stop making them work so hard, and to give them straw to make bricks.

Pharaoh told them, "You're all just lazy, that's why you ask for days off to serve Hashem. Nothing will change! Go back to work."

They left, discouraged and hopeless.

And on that very day, Moshe came back to Egypt.

A group of Jews met Moshe and Aharon. "Look what you've done!" they said bitterly to Moshe. "Because of you, Pharaoh hates us even more than he did before you came. Since you came, things have gotten a lot worse."

Moshe and Aharon were silent. What could they say?

Moshe Talks to Hashem

The complaints of the Jewish foremen made Moshe very sad. It hurt him that he was the cause of Jewish suffering. He prayed to Hashem and asked him, "Why did You send me? I only made things worse."

Hashem assured him, "Just wait and see what I'll do to Pharaoh."

QUESTIONS, ANYONE?

If Pharaoh wanted to make the Jews work harder, why didn't he command them to make more bricks each day? Why come up with such a strange plan, that they would have to find their own straw?

This way Pharaoh would not only hurt their bodies, but he could hurt their minds as well. He would drive them crazy with worry. They had to find their own straw. This meant that instead of being able to get a good night's sleep after work, they would be up all night worrying, "Where will I get straw tomorrow? Where can I go, what should I do?" That was much worse than having to make extra bricks.

פָּרָשַׁת וָאֵרָא

✦
Parashas
Va'eira

Va'eira · וָאֵרָא

Parashah Pointers

▸ Moshe gives the Jews a message from Hashem: Hashem is taking them out of Egypt!

▸ Moshe and Aharon tell Pharaoh that Hashem commands that he send out the Jews. Pharaoh asks for a miracle to prove that Hashem sent them. Aharon throws the walking stick to the ground and it turns into a snake.

▸ Pharaoh's wizards turn their sticks into snakes. Aharon's snake turns into a stick and swallows the wizards' snakes.

▸ Hashem punishes the Egyptians with seven of the Ten Makkos — Plagues. (The last three are in the next parashah.)

▸   1. דָּם, Blood: The waters of the Nile River turn into blood. So does every drop of water in all of Egypt. Only the Jews have clear water to drink.

▸   2. צְפַרְדֵּעַ, Frogs: Frogs come out of the river and cover the whole land of Egypt. The frogs get into the homes, food, even the bodies of the Egyptians.

▸   3. כִּנִּים, Lice: Lice crawl all over the Egyptians, making them itch and scratch all the time.

▸   4. עָרוֹב, Wild Animals: Wild animals wander throughout Egypt. They frighten the Egyptians, enter their homes, and attack the people.

▸   5. דֶּבֶר, Epidemic (or Sickness): The Egyptians' cows, sheep, camels, donkeys, and horses become sick and die.

▸   6. שְׁחִין, Boils: The Egyptians' skin is covered in painful boils and blisters.

▸   7. בָּרָד, Hail: A gigantic, icy hailstorm hits Egypt. Inside these icy hailstones is fire! The fiery hailstones cause great damage to Egypt's crops, animals, and people.

Great Things Are Happening

ast week's parashah ended with Moshe complaining to Hashem that things had become worse since he had come to Egypt. Hashem told him to just wait and see what happens.

Now, Hashem tells Moshe to go tell the Jews all the great things He will do for them.

"I promise to take you out (וְהוֹצֵאתִי) from having to work for the Egyptians. I will rescue you (וְהִצַּלְתִּי) from slavery. I will free you (וְגָאַלְתִּי) with powerful miracles. I will take you (וְלָקַחְתִּי) to be My nation and I will be your G-d, and I will bring you (וְהֵבֵאתִי) to the land that I promised to give to Avraham, Yitzchak, and Yaakov."

Moshe ran to tell the Jews Hashem's message. You would think this news would make them dance with joy. They were going to be free! But that's not what happened. The Jews were working too hard to listen to Moshe. Instead, they stayed gloomy and sad. They were broken, tired, and depressed by their hard work. They had just given up hope of ever getting out of Egypt.

Hashem then spoke to Moshe, "Tell Pharaoh to let the Jews leave Egypt." Moshe answered, "Pharaoh won't listen to me. Even the Jews didn't listen to me. And besides, I can't speak clearly."

"Aharon will go with you and he will do the talking," Hashem replied. Then He spoke to both Moshe and Aharon. "Go tell Pharaoh to let the Jews go.* When he asks you to prove that I sent you, tell Aharon to throw down the walking stick before Pharaoh. It will turn into a snake."

The Big Joke

nce again Moshe and Aharon stood in Pharaoh's throne room and spoke to the little man on the big throne. Moshe said to Pharaoh, "Let my people go."

Pharaoh answered, just as Hashem said he would, "Do something miraculous to prove that Hashem sent you."

Aharon threw the walking stick to the floor. Miraculously, it turned into a snake, hissing and sliding back and forth on the floor. Its head lifted up as it looked for someone to bite into with its poisonous fangs. What a frightening sight!

You would think that Pharaoh and his guards would have been terrified. But they weren't scared at all. They just laughed.

---

* Even though Moshe was told in the last parashah that Aharon would speak for him, that was to the Jews only. Now Hashem added that Aharon would speak for Moshe to Pharaoh as well.

Hashem promised to *take out*, *rescue*, and *free* the Jews. He would then *take* them as His people. Why did Hashem use many different words to say the same thing — that *He* would take the Jews out of Egypt?

Hashem didn't free the Jews all at once. Each of the different words He used was a promise for a separate step that He would take to free them.

First: Their slave labor would stop. They would completely stop working for the Egyptians.

Second: They would leave Egypt.

Third: Even if the Jews would leave Egypt, they were afraid that Egypt would force them back into slavery. After the miracle of Kriyas Yam Suf, the Jews knew that wouldn't happen.

Fourth: The final step. The Jews would get the Torah at Sinai.

To remind us of these four expressions of freedom, we drink four cups of wine on Seder night.

Torah in our Lives

Why did Hashem tell Aharon and not Moshe to hit the river with his stick in the makkos of blood and of frogs?

This is because of hakaras hatov. Hakaras hatov means gratitude. It means that when someone does something good for you, you show appreciation and say thank you, and of course you should not do anything bad to that person.

The Nile River saved baby Moshe's life. Moshe's mother hid him in a box and put it in the river to save him from the Egyptian police who would have killed him. Because of that, it would have been wrong for Moshe to harm the water that had saved him. Even though the water has no feelings, Hashem is showing us the right way to behave.

For the same reason, Moshe did not hit the earth to turn it into lice. Moshe had used the earth to hide the Egyptian he had killed, so he should not harm it.

If someone does us a favor, we thank them and show them that we are grateful.

How?

The first step is to say thank you. When we leave a restaurant, we thank the waiter. We say thanks to our bus driver or the mother who drove carpool.

Even more than that is to be kind and nice to the person who did you a favor. Do you have an older sister or brother who helps you with your homework or cheers you up when you have a fight with your best friend? Be nice to them. You have an aunt and uncle who give you birthday gifts? Give them a call and say hello.

"This is a sign?!" said Pharaoh. "In Egypt anyone can do this magic." Egypt, at that time, was a center of sorcery. Many Egyptians could do magic — even children!

Pharaoh brought some schoolchildren into the throne room and said to them, "Turn your sticks into snakes." And they did!

Pharaoh then called his queen. The queen also let her stick fall and it became a snake.

Then Pharaoh's chief wizards, Yochani and Mamrei, did the same with their sticks. They also made fun of Moshe.

Not Funny!

All the Egyptians were laughing. But not for long!

By now the floor was covered with snakes. Aharon's snake lowered its head to the ground. Its body became stiff and suddenly it changed back into a stick. Then ... the stick began to move as if it were alive! One by one, Aharon's stick swallowed all the snakes.

The Egyptians stopped laughing. This was something they couldn't do! Pharaoh was scared. "What if Aharon tells the stick to swallow me and my throne?" he wondered.

And yet Pharaoh didn't give in. Pharaoh was stubborn and hardened his heart to say: "No, they are not leaving!"

Bloody River

The Torah now begins telling us about the miracles of the Ten Makkos — the ten strange, terrifying, and awesome plagues that Hashem brought on the Egyptians.

Dam — Blood

Hashem sent Moshe and Aharon to meet Pharaoh by the Nile River. They reminded him that when they told him to let the Jews go, he didn't obey. Now Hashem would turn the Nile River to "dam," to blood. The fish would die, the river would smell horrible, and no one would be able to drink its water!

That would teach Pharaoh Who Hashem is!

Later, in front of Pharaoh and his servants, Aharon lifted the stick. He stretched it over Egypt's waters — the rivers and lakes. Then, with a huge splash, he brought his stick down and hit the Nile River — and all the water in Egypt turned to blood!

But the water of the Jews didn't.

If all the water in Egypt changed to blood, where did Pharaoh's wizards get water to turn into blood?

Only drinkable water turned to blood. The wizards used undrinkable, salty sea water to turn into blood, or they bought water from the Jews.

FASCINATING FACTS

Not only did Egypt's water turn to blood, but here, there, and everywhere in Egypt blood was dripping.

It dripped from the fruits, the trees, the walls of their homes, and from the mouths of the Egyptians.

The big stone idols in the streets and public buildings had blood dripping from their faces.

Each of the makkos lasted for seven days, except for two: Makkas Choshech (the Plague of Darkness) took six days and Makkas Bechoros (the Plague of the Firstborn) was one night. There was one makkah every month.

Pharaoh turned to his wizards and asked them if they could change water to blood. They took water and used magic to change the water to blood.

Seeing this, Pharaoh decided not to obey Hashem's command.

PANIC!

1magine going to get a cup of water, and blood comes out of the faucet. You run to your neighbor for help, but his water has turned to blood too. What's going on?

Both of you run to a nearby river. What do you see? As far as the eye can see, for miles and miles, the water in the river has changed from bluish-green to deep, blood red.

You get closer and see dead fish floating on the river. There is a terrible smell in the air everywhere. All around you thousands of people are trying to drink the river's water and spitting it out. It's blood!

You would totally panic!

That is what was happening all over Egypt. The Egyptians frantically asked each other: "Where can we get water?"

And then they saw their slaves. Imagine: Those Jews had cups that were filled with beautiful, clear water. And they were drinking it!

Thirsty, frightened, and angry, the Egyptians grabbed the cups from them.

And that beautiful water turned to blood.

Nothing worked. Even if a Jew and an Egyptian drank from the same cup at the same time, the Jew got water, the Egyptian got blood.

Seven Days

Makkas Dam lasted seven days. No one can last that long without water. So how did the Egyptians survive? There was only one way to get water. They had to *buy* it from the Jews. Only water bought from the Jews did not turn to blood.

Tz'fardei'a — Frogs

Ribbit, Ribbit

Hashem said to Moshe, "Go warn Pharaoh: If you don't let My people go, you will be hit with frogs."

Pharaoh ignored the warning.

דָּם

צְפַרְדֵּעַ

QUESTIONS, ANYONE?

Why did Hashem punish the Egyptians with frogs?

Egyptians would torture the Jews by making them catch roaches, worms, snails, and other disgusting bugs.

FASCINATING FACTS

There were brave frogs who chose to jump into hot ovens, to ruin the bread the Egyptians were baking. Though the ovens were hot enough to kill the frogs, they jumped in anyway.

What was their reward for risking their lives? At the end of the makkah, when all the frogs in Egypt died, these brave frogs stayed alive, hopping happily back into the Nile.

Moshe told Aharon to once again stretch his walking stick over Egypt's waters. A huge frog jumped out of the water. It started loudly screeching, "Ribbit, ribbit." The Egyptians began hitting it. Every time they beat it an army of frogs jumped out of the big frog. The frog army then hopped their way to Pharaoh's palace.

The guards saw this mass of frogs and slammed the palace doors shut. That didn't stop the frogs. They went underground and came up through the palace floor.

How did soft, squishy frogs get through the stone and marble tiles of the palace floor? The frogs croaked, "Let us through! Hashem sent us!" The floor split and let the frogs through.

Attack!

From Pharaoh's palace the frog army spread out all over Egypt. They went everywhere and went into everything. There was only one place where there were no frogs. That was the neighborhood where the Jews lived — Goshen.

The frogs covered the ground and jumped into homes. Although the Egyptians tried their best to keep the frogs out, the frogs managed to get inside, and they got into everything.

Not only were the frogs everywhere, but they jumped on the Egyptians and bit them. Frogs jumped into the Egyptians' food. When they poured a cup of wine, frogs would suddenly jump in. Frogs were in their stomachs and in their mouths. They were in their beds, on the tables and chairs. They hopped in as the Egyptians kneaded dough to make bread, and they even risked their lives to jump into the fiery ovens.

All those frogs croaked and croaked, making it so noisy no one could hear what anyone else was saying, unless they yelled. Between the noise and the frogs jumping all over the bed, who could sleep?

Be Gone!

"Enough!" said Pharaoh to his advisers. "I can't take the frogs anymore. They are driving me crazy! Get Moshe and Aharon. Tell them to come to the palace."

When they arrived Pharaoh begged them, "Pray to Hashem to take away the frogs, and I will let the Jews go."

Moshe davened to Hashem and all the frogs died (except for the ones that had jumped into the oven!).

But Pharaoh didn't keep his promise.

The frogs were gone but the Jews were

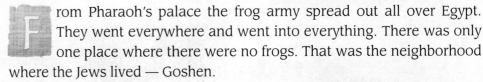

forced to remain in Egypt.

The Egyptians began removing dead frogs from their homes and fields. What a major clean-up job! All over Egypt were huge piles of dead frogs — four piles of dead frogs for every Egyptian. There was an awful smell from the dead frogs.

Kinim — Lice

Itching and Scratching

Lice are horrid. The tiny little bugs get into people's hair and make them scratch and scratch and scratch. And they are so hard to get rid of! There are also lice that crawl all over the body and it itches.

Because the Egyptians made the Jews sweep the dust in their houses and in the streets, Hashem punished them by turning their dust into lice — kinim. But there were no lice in Goshen. Jews were not itching and scratching.

This is what happened:

Hashem said to Moshe, "Tell Aharon to stretch out the stick and hit the dust of the land." Aharon did as Moshe told him. Suddenly, Egypt was full of lice, big ones and small ones. The land became covered with a layer of lice about two feet thick! The tiny bugs were hungry and went straight to find humans and animals to feed on.

The Egyptians felt something on their bodies and began to scratch. And scratch. And scratch. No matter how hard they tried they couldn't get rid of the little bugs in their hair and on their bodies. Some tried to scratch their backs on the walls, but all that happened was they scratched off their skin. Ouch!

Pharaoh suddenly felt itchy. He started to scratch. His hair, his beard (which was two feet long!), his nose — all over. All around him everyone was constantly scratching.

Pharaoh knew very well who'd brought these lice to his country. He called his wizards again. "Could they do this too?" he wondered. "Could they also create lice?"

The wizards came. But unlike the blood and frogs, no matter how hard they tried, they could not do what Moshe and Aharon had done. Magic could not make something as tiny as lice.

"This makkah is a finger of Hashem," they told Pharaoh.

Pharaoh didn't care. He still refused to let the Jews go.

TORAH IN OUR LIVES

Since more frogs came out every time the Egyptians hit the large frog, why did they keep on hitting it?

The Steipler Gaon explains that this shows us how people react when they get angry. They don't think clearly and do things only because they are upset. Sometimes a person is upset so he breaks a toy or something else he really likes.

Other times, small arguments become big fights because a person was angry. If one of the people had thought about it, he would have kept quiet and the argument would simply have ended. Instead, it got worse and worse until it became a terrible fight.

כנים

ערוב

Arov — Wild Animals

Warning: Danger Ahead

Hashem told Moshe to go to Pharaoh and tell him Hashem's next message: "Send My people out to worship Me. If not, your land and your homes will be filled with all kinds of wild animals. But where the Jews live in Goshen, there will be no wild animals. All this will happen so that you know that I am Hashem Who rules over the land."

Moshe warned Pharaoh, as Hashem had commanded. But Pharaoh was stubborn and didn't obey Hashem. As a result, the wild animals invaded Egypt.

Lions and Tigers and Bears

Imagine opening the door to your house one morning and finding yourself facing the open jaws of a roaring lion. You scream, turn around, and run. The lion chases you through the house. You make it out the back door and close it behind you. Whew, you're safe. Then you smell something funny. You turn around — what smells so bad? In front of you is an enormous elephant in your backyard.

That's what it was like during Makkas Arov.

Only worse. The Egyptians didn't escape the lions or any of the other wild animals that chased them.

Terror Everywhere

Along with ferocious beasts like lions, tigers, and bears, Hashem sent snakes and scorpions.

In a zoo, the animals are in cages and people walk free. But during this makkah the animals walked free and the people were locked in their homes. They were afraid to go out.

For seven days the animals terrorized Egypt. They broke into homes, went where they pleased, destroyed property, and attacked humans.

Except Jews. Jews could see giraffes, jaguars, and other animals wandering the streets where the Egyptians lived. But where the Jews lived everything was quiet and normal. No animals set foot — nor paws nor hooves! — on Jewish streets.

QUESTIONS, ANYONE?

Why did Hashem punish the Egyptians with wild animals?

Being invaded by ferocious beasts was what the Egyptians deserved, because they sent Jews out into dangerous places to capture wild animals for them.

QUESTIONS, ANYONE?

When Hashem stopped Makkas Arov, why didn't they die, like the frogs?

When the frogs died, they brought a terrible smell to all of Egypt. Also, getting rid of so many dead frogs was a headache. If Hashem would have let the animals die in Egypt, the Egyptians would have used the skins of the animals to make fancy fur coats for themselves and their wives. Hashem did not want them to have any benefit from the makkah, so the animals just disappeared. One moment they were in the streets, roaring and running around, and the next moment it was quiet. They were just gone.

Pharaoh Gives In

Moshe and Aharon were called to appear before Pharaoh. "I'll let you sacrifice to your Hashem here in Egypt," Pharaoh said.

"We can't do that," Moshe replied. "We sacrifice lambs and sheep to Hashem. These are animals that you Egyptians bow down to as gods. If people see us using their gods they will try to kill us. No, we want to leave for a three-day trip into the desert and serve Hashem there."

Pharaoh said, "All right, go. But don't go far. Now pray for me and take away the wild animals!"

"I'll pray to Hashem to remove the animals tomorrow. But don't change your mind about letting us go after the animals are gone!"

Moshe prayed and the animals disappeared. However, Pharaoh did not keep his promise. He did not let the Jews go.

Dever — The Animals Die

Another Warning

Once again Moshe went to Pharaoh to deliver Hashem's warning:

"Send out My people and if you don't, your animals will get sick and die. All the horses, donkeys, camels, cattle, and sheep that are out in the fields will die. But not one of the Jewish animals will die."

Once again Pharaoh didn't send out the Jews, and Makkas Dever — animals dying from disease — began.

Smart Egyptians

By now there were some Egyptians who had learned their lesson. They were afraid of the power of Hashem. They knew that if Moshe said something would happen, it would.

Moshe said that Hashem would kill the animals in the fields. So they brought all their animals into their homes to make sure they would be safe. And those animals didn't die.

But the other Egyptians? Their animals were in trouble.

An Egyptian was walking with his flock of sheep. He was a rich man who owned more than one hundred sheep. Suddenly he saw his sheep begin to fall and make terrible noises. They were very sick — all of them, at the same time. As the shepherd watched, his sheep's eyes closed. The entire flock was dead! Suddenly, the wealthy man was poor.

Another Egyptian was riding his camel. All of a sudden the camel stopped moving. The owner whipped the camel, but the camel wouldn't budge. The camel fell to the ground — dead — and his rider fell down and broke a leg. In some cases the animal fell, causing the rider to tumble off, break his neck, and die.

Pharaoh Is Desperate

Pharaoh tried to show that Moshe was a liar and wasn't really sent by Hashem. He figured that if all the animals were getting sick and dying, the Jewish animals would be dying too. An animal is an animal, what's the difference who its owner is?

Pharaoh sent his people to check if the Jewish animals were dying. They told Pharaoh that none of the Jewish animals had died. Pharaoh learned that Moshe told the truth!

But it didn't matter. Pharaoh still refused to let the Jews go.

FASCINATING FACTS

There were Egyptian animals that were left outside and yet they did not die.

Why?

Because they were owned by partners, a Jew and an Egyptian.

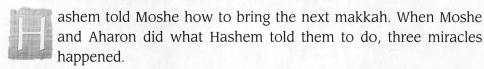

Shechin — Boils and Blisters

Three Miracles

Hashem told Moshe how to bring the next makkah. When Moshe and Aharon did what Hashem told them to do, three miracles happened.

Moshe reached into an oven with both hands and filled them with two handfuls of ashes. Aharon did the same. They stood before Pharaoh, their hands full of ashes. Pharaoh watched as Aharon took his ashes and put them on the ashes Moshe was holding in his hands. Though Moshe's hands had been full, all of Aharon's ashes fit in his hands. None of it spilled to the ground. That was the first miracle.

Take a handful of sand at the beach and throw it up in the air. It doesn't get very far. Moshe threw the ashes up into the air. It kept going up and up, higher and higher in the sky until it reached heaven. That was a second miracle.

Then came the third miracle. The ashes came down, and though it had been such a small amount — only a few handfuls — it miraculously spread out and fell all over Egypt.

The ashes caused terrible boils and blisters to break out all over the bodies of the Egyptians and their animals. Makkas Shechin had hit Egypt.

דֶּבֶר

שְׁחִין

בָּרָד

Boils and Blisters

B esides the terrible pain of being covered with boils and blisters, the Egyptians couldn't take a bath for a whole week! Because of the blisters, they would scream in pain whenever their skin would touch the bath water.

This was their punishment for screaming at their Jewish slaves to bring water from the river, cut wood, and make a fire to heat up the water. All that work, so their Egyptian masters could take a hot bath.

Barad — Hail

Severe Warning

H ashem sent a severe warning to Pharaoh, letting him know how he would be punished next.

Moshe told Pharaoh in the Name of Hashem: "There is no one like Me in the whole world. I could wipe you and your people out if I wanted to, just like I killed all the animals. But I want to keep you alive because you deserve to be punished and so I can show you My power. The whole world will hear about what happened to you and know that I am Hashem. You are still not letting My people go!"

Moshe then scratched a mark on the wall of Pharaoh's palace and said, "This time tomorrow, when the sun hits this mark, there will be a severe hailstone storm over all of Egypt. Take care that no people or animals are outside when the hail comes. Anyone caught in the storm will be killed by the hailstones."

Moshe finished speaking and walked out.

Balls of Fire and Ice

T he next day Moshe raised his stick and pointed it to the sky. There was loud thunder, and gigantic hailstones began to come down from the sky. Frozen balls of ice were falling on Egypt, a country that was burning hot and very dry. There are parts of Egypt where it hardly ever rains and it never snows. Not only that, but this wasn't a quick storm that came and went. The storm lasted seven days! It was a storm that Egypt — and the entire world — had never seen before.

But that wasn't all. An even greater miracle happened. Inside the balls of ice, there was fire. Fire and water never go together. Water puts out fire. But Hashem changed nature. The ice balls didn't put out the fire inside them, and the fire didn't melt the ice.

And there were more miracles to come ...

FASCINATING FACTS

Pharaoh's wizards had so many boils and blisters and were in so much pain, they couldn't even stand up. They suffered more than other Egyptians. Hashem punished them for telling Pharaoh to throw the newborn Jewish boys into the river.

___

In this world Hashem doesn't want people to be robots who have no choice except to do what they are programmed to do. He wants everyone to be able to choose whether to do right or wrong. That way, if they do good things, they will deserve to be rewarded.

After seeing all the miracles Moshe had done already, and how every makkah happened just as he had said, of course Pharaoh would see how powerful Hashem is, and would agree to send the Jews out.

So to make things even and fair, Hashem hardened Pharaoh's heart enough so that if he really wanted to do evil, he could. It would be up to him to decide if he would listen to Hashem. He did bad things because he was a bad person.

Imagine

Imagine being in a sudden rainstorm. Everyone around you is getting wet, except for one person. Everyone else is getting soaked, but he is perfectly dry. (And no, he doesn't have an umbrella!) It's raining everywhere, on everyone — but not on him.

That's what happened to the Egyptians. Here is this scary hailstorm, with balls of fire and ice falling everywhere. Yet the sun is shining wherever there is a Jew.

Where the Jews live, there is no hail. Just sunshine.

FASCINATING FACTS

The Barad wiped out all the food growing in Egypt, except the fields of wheat and spelt that were not ripe yet. Hashem saved them so that they would be destroyed in the next makkah, eaten by locusts.

Damage

The hail came down and smashed trees. Then the ice balls broke apart and the fire inside burned the trees. Nothing was left but burnt-out trees. The fires spread and did even more damage to fields and property.

There were Egyptians who were not afraid of Hashem, and they did not stay safely inside. They and their animals were killed when they got hit by the hailstones.

The Egyptians never got to eat the meat of their dead animals. Hashem sent birds to eat the dead animals before the Egyptians could take them home to eat.

"I Sinned"

Pharaoh called for Moshe and Aharon to come. When they got there he told them something you would never have expected to hear. "I have sinned," he said. "Hashem is a Tzaddik and I and my people are wicked. Pray to Hashem to stop the thunder and hail and I will let everyone go."

Sounds like Pharaoh finally did teshuvah, right? But Moshe knew it wasn't so.

"You don't fool me," he said. "I know that when the Barad stops you won't let us go. You are still not afraid of Hashem, Who is G-d."

Moshe went out and raised his hands to heaven and prayed. The thunder stopped. The balls of ice stopped falling from the sky — they stayed in mid-air!

But Moshe was right. As soon as the hail stopped, Pharaoh broke his promise and didn't let the Jews go.

פָּרָשַׁת בֹּא

·

Parashas Bo

Bo · בֹּא

Parashah Pointers

▸ Hashem sends two more makkos:

8. **אַרְבֶּה**, Locusts: Super-hungry, big grasshoppers, called locusts, invade Egypt. They eat everything that grows.

9. **חֹשֶׁךְ**, Darkness: Although it is daytime, Egypt suddenly gets dark — very, very dark — for six days.

▸ Pharaoh says he will let the Jews go, but not their animals. Moshe answers that all the Jews must leave, with their animals too! Pharaoh tells Moshe never to come to him again!

▸ The Jews are given their first mitzvah — to declare the first day of the new month as Rosh Chodesh.

▸ Moshe instructs the Jews to bring the Korban Pesach.

▸ Hashem gives the Jews the laws of Pesach.

▸ The Jews are sitting and eating their Korban Pesach, matzah, and maror. At midnight, the tenth makkah strikes.

▸ 10. **מַכַּת בְּכוֹרוֹת**, Plague of the Firstborn: All over Egypt, all firstborn men, women, and animals die.

▸ Pharaoh tells Moshe and Aharon that the Jews are free to go. Moshe says, "We will leave in the morning."

▸ Millions of Jews leave Egypt in a grand, awesome parade.

▸ The Jews take their leftover matzah and maror. They leave Egypt in such a hurry that their dough doesn't have time to rise, and it turns into matzah.

▸ Hashem gives the Jews more mitzvos.

1. **Pidyon Haben:** A boy who is a woman's firstborn is a bechor. His father redeems him by giving five shekels of silver to a Kohen when he is thirty days old.

2. **Kiddush Bechor Beheimah:** A male firstborn sheep, goat, or cow is holy. It is given to a Kohen for a korban (offering).

3. **Pidyon Petter Chamor:** A firstborn male donkey can't be used until the owner gives a sheep or goat to the Kohen to redeem it.

4. **Sippur Yetzias Mitzrayim:** On Seder night we tell how the Jews were slaves in Egypt and Hashem freed them.

5. **Tefillin**: Men are to put on tefillin every day except Shabbos and Yom Tov.

Pharaoh Tries to Bargain

Hashem tells Moshe to go warn Pharaoh that if he doesn't let the Jews go, He will send another makkah, of locusts. (Locusts are a type of big, hungry grasshoppers.) For the first time, Pharaoh is not so stubborn. When Moshe and Aharon warn him about the next makkah, he doesn't absolutely refuse to send out the Jews.

Instead, he wants to "make a deal" with Moshe. He will agree to send out only some Jews. But Pharaoh will learn that you don't bargain with Hashem. You do what He says.

Moshe and Aharon told Pharaoh, "Hashem, the G-d of the Jews, says: 'You refuse to be humble and obey Me. Because you won't send out My people, I will send locusts to invade Egypt.' "

Moshe saw Pharaoh's ministers whispering to each other. It seemed that this time they would tell Pharaoh to let the Jews go. So Moshe stopped talking and left the throne room. He wanted to give Pharaoh's ministers a chance to speak to the king. Maybe they would persuade him to let the Jews go.

When Moshe left, Pharaoh's ministers told him, "Let them go and serve their G-d. Don't you realize that if you don't, Egypt will be destroyed?"

Pharaoh decided they were right.

FASCINATING FACTS

Nowadays, when locusts swarm, there can be at least 80 million and sometimes as many as 160 million locusts in a square mile! And the plague of locusts in Egypt was much worse!

Throw Them Out!

He called Moshe and Aharon back and asked, "Who will be going?" Moshe answered, "It's a Yom Tov for us. All of us will go, including the young and the old. We will take our animals with us, as well."

"There is no way I'm sending the children. Only the men can go!" Pharaoh shouted.

Pharaoh was still stubborn. So Hashem punished the Egyptians with yet another makkah.

Arbeh — Locusts

Locusts!

Moshe stretched out his stick over Egypt. A powerful eastern wind began to blow. It was blowing locusts into Egypt.

There were billions of them! They covered the earth and the sky. Even though it was midday, it was dark in Egypt, because the locusts blocked out the sun. It was terrifying. The

Along with the locusts Hashem sent poisonous snakes to bite and kill the Egyptians.

The Egyptians had forced the Jews to plant fields of wheat and barley, so the locusts came and ate their crops.

Pharaoh said he sinned "to Hashem and to you," meaning Moshe and Aharon. It's clear he had sinned to Hashem by not sending the Jews out. But how had he sinned to Moshe and Aharon?

The last time they had come to him he had thrown them out of the throne room. This is not the way to treat a visitor. Now he apologized.

locusts were very hungry. They ate any plants and crops that were growing.

Not only were the locusts in the field, they also filled the Egyptians' homes. There were locusts on the walls, locusts on the tables, locusts everywhere. When the Egyptians opened their closets they found insects munching on their clothes.

Big Trouble

By now the Egyptians had very little to eat. Most of their animals had died in Makkas Dever, when the animals died of disease. The hail had destroyed most of the fruit trees and other crops. Whatever wasn't destroyed by the hail was now eaten by the locusts. The Egyptians were in big trouble — hardly any food could be found.

Finally: "I Have Sinned"

The situation was desperate. Pharaoh called Moshe and Aharon back to get rid of the locusts.

For the first time, Pharaoh admitted, "I have sinned to Hashem your G-d and to you. Please forgive my sin and pray to Hashem to take away the locusts."

Go!

Moshe prayed that the locusts should go away. Hashem sent a powerful wind from the west and it blew all the locusts to the Yam Suf (Sea of Reeds). Not only the live ones, but even the dead locusts that the Egyptians had salted and put aside to eat were miraculously blown away.

Choshech — Darkness

Number Nine

Hashem hardened Pharaoh's heart. He did not let the Jews go.

It was time for the ninth makkah — Makkas Choshech.

It was a beautiful, sunny day in Egypt when Moshe stretched his hand toward heaven. Suddenly there was darkness. It was as if someone had turned off the sun. No moon or stars — just blackness everywhere. It was as if everyone in Egypt had become blind.

The darkness was even darker than the blackness you "see" when you close your eyes in a dark room right before going to sleep. People could not even see the person next to them.

Everyone was moving very slowly. The Egyptians walked with hands outstretched, trying not to bump into trees, or stumble and fall, or fall

אַרְבֶּה

חֹשֶׁךְ

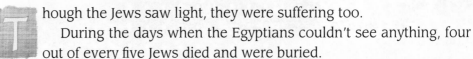

down stairs. They tried lighting candles and fires to be able to see, but nothing happened. The candles and fires went out.

For three days the Egyptians didn't see the sun and couldn't see anything.

Tragedy

Though the Jews saw light, they were suffering too.

During the days when the Egyptians couldn't see anything, four out of every five Jews died and were buried.

Who were they? Why did they die?

These were Jews who wanted to stay in Egypt. Many of them were wealthy because the Egyptians rewarded them for being good workers. Some had been put in charge of forcing other Jews to work. Hashem was punishing them, but He didn't want the Egyptians to realize that Jews are also being punished. That's why He caused these people to die when the Egyptians couldn't see. The Egyptians would never know what had happened.

Can't Move!

After the third day, the darkness got even thicker. It wasn't like normal darkness anymore. It was like a very thick and black fog. It was so thick that no one could move for three whole days.

If an Egyptian was standing when the darkness got worse, that was it — he stood for three days straight, not moving. Some Egyptians froze while bending over or in mid-step. They stayed frozen that way for three days!

Footsteps in the Darkness

During these three days of thick darkness, the Jews who had been their slaves were there searching for gold, silver, jewelry, and expensive clothes. Even though the house was dark for the Egyptians, for the Jews there was light. The Egyptians, frozen in their chairs, beds, or wherever they'd been, couldn't stop the Jews from searching their homes. But the Jews did not take anything, even though no one could stop them. That would be stealing!

Instead, the Jews kept a record of what they found in the homes of their Egyptian bosses. That list would come in handy before they left Egypt. Hashem said that when the time came for the Jews to leave, they should ask their neighbors for gold and jewelry. Of course, the

QUESTIONS, ANYONE?

Why were the Egyptians punished with darkness?

Because when the Egyptians traveled at night they made the Jews carry torches for them to light up the dark roads.

Also, when the Egyptians would eat at night, they would force a Jew to sit there with a candle on his head, like a human chandelier, so the Egyptian could have light.

They used the Jews to give them light, so Hashem punished them by taking away their light!

Egyptian would say, "Me? I'm not rich. I'm just a poor guy." That's when the Jew would take out the list he made during Makkas Choshech. He would look at it and say, "And what about the gold necklace in your bottom drawer, two diamond rings in the clothes closet? And let's not forget the solid silver bowl on your living-room table."

The Egyptian would then go and gather all the items on the list and give it to the Jew.

Get Out of Here!

The makkah was over. Pharaoh and his people could move again. As soon as he could, Pharaoh sent for Moshe and Aharon.

"Go worship Hashem and take your children with you," he told them. "But the animals must stay here in Egypt!"

Moshe answered, "Not only are we going with all our animals, but in the end, you will even give us animals as offerings to Hashem."

Pharaoh became stubborn again. "What chutzpah!" Pharaoh thought. "How dare he talk to me, the king of Egypt, that way!"

"Get out of here!" he shouted. "Beware, don't you dare come back. On the day you come and see my face, I will have you killed."

Pharaoh didn't scare Moshe and Aharon with his threats.

"What you said is true. I will never see your face in your palace again," Moshe told him.

> **FASCINATING FACTS**
>
> During Makkas Choshech it wasn't dark for the Jews — even at night.

Makkas Bechoros — Plague of the Firstborn

The Last Warning

Suddenly something happened to Moshe that had never happened before. Hashem spoke to him while he was standing in front of Pharaoh in the throne room! Moshe told Hashem's message to Pharaoh. "Hashem says: 'I will go through Egypt about midnight and every firstborn will die. From the firstborn of Pharaoh, the most important firstborn in the land, to the least important, the firstborn of servants and prisoners. All of them will die, and so will the firstborn animals. The sounds of so many people screaming and crying over their dead relatives will be very loud. It will be a sound that was never heard before in Egypt, and will never be heard again.'"

In a loud voice, so everyone there would hear him, Moshe said, "You were right when you told me not to come here anymore. Because the next time we meet, it won't be here — you will come to me!"

FASCINATING FACTS

When Moshe said the important people in the palace would bow to him, he meant Pharaoh as well. But out of respect for the king he didn't mention him.

Moshe then said, "This officer and this minister and everyone who lives in the palace will come with you and bow down to me and beg us to leave."

By this time all the Egyptian people, and even Pharaoh's ministers, realized that Moshe was a great man. They showed him respect and honor.

Revolution!

Word got out that the firstborn were going to die in the next makkah. Who was the most upset about the news? The firstborn people, of course! They didn't want to die. They spoke to their parents and spoke to Pharaoh. "Let the Jews go!" they said. "We want to live!"

But no one listened. Those who were not firstborn didn't care. They weren't going to die. Having no choice, the firstborn picked up their weapons and declared war against Pharaoh and his armies. In this battle thousands of Egyptians were killed even before Makkas Bechoros happened!

The First Mitzvah

Fifteen days before the Jews were going to leave Egypt, something incredibly exciting happened: The nation got its first mitzvah!

Hashem told Moshe and Aharon to look up. In the sky above them, they could see a very thin sliver of the moon.

Hashem instructed them to tell the Jews that when they see the moon start looking like that, that day is the beginning of the new month — Rosh Chodesh.

From then on the Jewish calendar would be based on the new moon. The time it takes for the moon to circle the earth once is a Jewish month.

In order that we always remember the miracle of leaving Egypt, G-d commanded that the month we left Egypt, Nissan, should be counted as the first month of our calendar.

Four Days to Go!

The tenth day of Nissan that year was Shabbos. Jews were commanded to take a young goat or lamb and tie it to their beds for four days. During that time they would make sure the animal did not have a flaw, so that it could be a korban to Hashem. That animal would be their Korban Pesach.

All the Jews had to do was to take a lamb, tie it up, and keep an eye on it. Sounds easy? It wasn't!

The Egyptians worshiped sheep and goats as gods. Imagine what courage it took for a Jew to go into a store and buy a sheep. "What are you buying it for?" the owner would ask. The Jew would answer, "To kill it as a korban to Hashem, and eat it." Imagine what the Egyptian seller would want to do to this Jew, who dared to plan to kill his god, and roast it too!

Although it was hard and even seemed dangerous, the Jews did as Hashem commanded. Amazingly, nothing happened to the Jews, because Hashem protected them.

For four days the Egyptians heard their "gods" going baaa, baaa, baaa, in Jewish homes — and they could do nothing about it.

Two Mitzvos

In order for the Jews to deserve to leave Egypt, Hashem gave them two mitzvos — and so they earned the right to leave Egypt.

Every Jew must be part of a group that would bring and eat the korban. It could be family or a group of friends. After shechitah, the animal should be roasted over a fire.

The second mitzvah was bris milah.

In order to eat the Korban Pesach, the men and boys had to have a bris milah. This was the second mitzvah. It takes courage for a grown person to have a bris. But Hashem said to do it, so they did!

No Chametz

Moshe taught the Jews all about the mitzvos of Pesach. These mitzvos included eating matzah and maror and getting rid of all chametz.

(For more on the mitzvos of Pesach, go to page 58.)

Moshe told them that at midnight before Yetzias Mitzrayim (the Exodus), Makkas Bechoros would strike Egypt. He assured them that the Jews would have nothing to worry about. As long as they smeared the blood of the Korban Pesach on their doorposts and stayed inside their homes, their firstborn would be safe.

Finally, Moshe told them the best news of all — on the very next morning, they would be leaving Egypt for good!

Protection

Hashem told Moshe what the Jews should do to protect themselves from Makkas Bechoros.

They should do the following:

▸ Catch some of the blood from the Korban Pesach in a dish.

▸ Take three twigs from a hyssop plant and tie them together. Dip the bundle into the blood.

▸ Go to the door of your house and, using the twigs as a brush, smear the blood on one doorpost.

▸ Dip again and smear on the other doorpost.

▸ Dip again, reach up, and smear the top of the doorway.

FASCINATING FACTS

The Shabbos before Pesach is called Shabbos HaGadol, the Great Shabbos. Why? One of the reasons is to remind us of the miracle that took place on the Shabbos before the first Pesach, when the Jews tied up their lambs and Hashem didn't let the Egyptians stop them.

———

When the Beis HaMikdash stood, the most important part of the Seder was the Korban Pesach. When Mashiach comes, we will all bring the korban again.

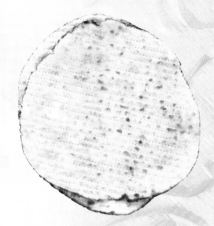

מַכַּת בְּכוֹרוֹת

Why "Pesach"?

The Hebrew word for "skipped over" is "pasach." We call the Yom Tov "Pesach" to remember how Hashem "skipped over" our homes when the Egyptian firstborn were dying. In English, it's called Passover for the same reason: because Hashem "passed over" the Jewish homes.

The Last Night

In all the Jewish homes, families were doing the mitzvos of Pesach. With their belts and shoes on, and their sticks in their hands — as if they were about to leave — they ate matzah and maror. The main thing on the table was a whole roasted lamb — the Korban Pesach. They ate from it, and got ready to leave Egypt.

Midnight

Suddenly, exactly at midnight, they heard loud, terrifying sounds. People were screaming and crying. The Jews knew that these were the sounds of Egyptians wailing over their dead relatives. It was the sound of Hashem punishing the Egyptians for making the Jews suffer horribly as slaves; for all the Jews who died of overwork or were killed by their Egyptian masters; for all the children they threw into the river.

Finally, the Egyptians were being punished for their evil! They wanted to kill the Jews, who are called "Hashem's firstborn." So Hashem killed their firstborn.

Hashem Himself

ashem Himself — not an angel — went through Egypt, killing the firstborn men and women. If a house had no firstborn sons, the oldest man in the house was killed. Even the firstborn of the prisoners and animals died! As He had promised, Hashem "passed over" the homes that had blood on the doorpost. In the Jewish homes, everyone was safe.

Ice Cream!

The Egyptians watched as their metal idols suddenly melted, like ice cream in the desert sun. Wooden idols rotted. Hashem destroyed their idols so that the Egyptians would finally understand that only Hashem is G-d.

In the Palace

haraoh had gone to bed that night but now he was up. His firstborn son was dead. All over the palace there were dead people. Instead of blaming himself for not letting the Jews go, Pharaoh blamed his advisers. It was their fault, he said, for not telling him to let the Jews go. In his anger, he picked up his sword and killed one adviser after another.

They got what they deserved for advising Pharaoh to throw the Jewish boys into the river.

Where Is He?

nce the makkah began, Pharaoh and the Egyptians were terrified they would all die if they didn't get Moshe to stop it. Though it was the middle of the night, Pharaoh himself ran around gathering his ministers, generals, and other important people to go with him to find Moshe and Aharon.

They went to where the Jews lived. A panicked Pharaoh screamed, "Where do Moshe and Aharon live? Where are they?"

No Jew went out to help Pharaoh. They couldn't. Hashem had warned them not to step outside all that night. But hearing Pharaoh's voice, the Jews looked out their windows. There was Pharaoh surrounded by his servants holding torches, so he could see where to go in the dark.

Pharaoh ran everywhere looking for Moshe and Aharon. The Jews kept pointing in different directions, sending Pharaoh back and forth.

Look at what had become of the great and mighty Pharaoh!

FASCINATING FACTS

There were Egyptians who tried to save themselves by sleeping in Jewish homes. It didn't help; they died too.

———

Every Erev Pesach, firstborn men and boys are supposed to fast. This is called Taanis Bechoros. If a firstborn boy is less than 13 years old, his father fasts for him.

However, a firstborn who has been at a mitzvah-meal (such as a bris or siyum) may eat. That is why there is a custom for someone to make a siyum in shul after Shacharis on Erev Pesach.

"YOU ARE FREE"

inally, they found Moshe. Pharaoh and all his generals and ministers bowed low to the ground before Moshe, begging for mercy, just as Moshe had predicted.

"Please go!" Pharaoh said.

"Now? In the middle of the night?" Moshe answered. "Are we thieves who sneak out in middle of the night? We will go in the morning in broad daylight, so everyone will see that we didn't sneak out. They will see that we walked out and you did not stop us."

Pharaoh pleaded with Moshe, "But I am a firstborn. If you don't leave now I'm afraid I'll die. All of Egypt may die if you stay."

Moshe said, "It's up to you to stop the makkah." He then told Pharaoh exactly what he had to do.

Pharaoh went through the streets and yelled, so all the Jews could hear, "You are free, you are free! Take your children, your animals, everything — and go!" That's why Pharaoh was allowed to live.

A Special Night of Miracles

The night of Yetzias Mitzrayim (the Exodus), the 15th of Nissan, is a very special one. Throughout Jewish history, incredible miracles have happened on that night. Here are some of the times when our enemies were defeated or Jews were saved from destruction on the Seder night:

Way before Yetzias Mitzrayim, Avraham Avinu fought the huge armies of *four* kings and won! How big was Avraham's army? It was just Avraham and his loyal servant, Eliezer. It seems that two people against four armies are enough — when it's time for a miracle.

Yaakov fought all night with the evil angel of Eisav, who wanted to kill him. Though it was a battle between a human and an angel, Yaakov won.

The city of Yerushalayim was surrounded by the huge Assyrian army who were ready to attack. Then Hashem sent an angel that wiped out the whole Assyrian army. The morning after the Seder, the Jews found the Assyrian soldiers were dead! The Jews had won — without lifting a finger.

The Babylonian Empire under King Nevuchadnetzar had destroyed the First Beis HaMikdash and sent the Jews into exile. Years later, Nevuchadnetzar's grandson Baalshatzar became king of Babylon. An evil man, he made a party on the Seder night, and had the chutzpah to drink from the cups his grandfather stole from the Beis HaMikdash. That same night Baalshatzar's palace was invaded. He was killed and the Babylonian Empire came to an end.

Daniel was thrown into a cave with hungry lions as punishment for praying to Hashem. He spent the Seder night with the lions — who left him unharmed. In the morning he was freed.

Achashveirosh commanded Haman to lead Mordechai through the streets of Shushan on the king's horse. That was the beginning of the end of Haman.

Preparing to Leave

Hashem told Moshe, "I will keep My promise to Avraham, that after the Jews suffer in slavery I will free them. They will be wealthy. Tell the Jews to ask the Egyptians for their gold and silver and nice clothing."

The Jews did as Hashem told them. They went from house to house asking their Egyptian neighbors to give them their wealth. The Jews knew exactly what to ask for, because during Makkas Choshech they had searched the homes of the Egyptians to see where they kept their valuables.

Because the Jewish slaves had worked hard for so many years without being paid, they had a right to take all that money.

FASCINATING FACTS

When the Jews finally arrived in Eretz Yisrael, they buried Yosef in the city of Shechem. That is the place where his brothers sold him as a slave.

Yosef

Before he died, Yosef asked the Jews to swear that when they would leave Egypt they would take his bones with them and bury them in Eretz Yisrael. Finally, the long-awaited moment was approaching. It was time to get Yosef's bones.

The Egyptians had put Yosef in a metal coffin and lowered it to the bottom of the Nile River. How would Moshe find Yosef's coffin, deep underwater? He didn't even know where it was.

Moshe went to the Nile and said, "Yosef, Yosef. The time has come to leave Egypt." Then he wrote Hashem's Name on a piece of pottery and threw it into the Nile. Suddenly, Yosef's coffin rose up from the bottom of the river and floated on the water. Moshe took the coffin with him, together with all the Jewish people!

Quickly, Quickly

he time had come to leave. The Jews packed up all the wealth they had gotten from the Egyptians. That came out to be ninety donkeys loaded with treasure … for each Jew!

They lovingly wrapped up the leftover matzah and maror from their Seder. It was so precious to them that they carried it themselves, instead of having it carried by the donkeys.

They prepared the dough to bake into bread. But leaving Egypt happened so quickly, the dough never had time to rise. It became matzah.

Emunah

hough the Jews knew they were going into the desert, they didn't prepare any food to take with them. They weren't worried about what they would eat in the dry desert, even though there

Usually, when dogs see strangers they bark. One of the miracles that happened when the Jews were leaving Egypt was the dogs didn't bark!

Hashem rewarded the dogs. How? Hashem said that if a Jew finds one of his animals has died, he should give its meat to a dog.

Now a dog is just a dog, not a human being who can make choices, and yet Hashem rewarded them for not barking. Imagine how much more we will be rewarded for doing mitzvos and being kind to others!

TORAH IN OUR LIVES

Hashem, in His great love for us, didn't take us out of Egypt in the summer, when we would broil and sweat in the heat. He didn't take us out in the winter when we would have gotten soaked and frozen traveling in the cold and rain. He took us out in the spring, when the weather is perfect for traveling, not too hot and not too cold!

He loved us then, and He loves us now. Through all the years that have passed, Hashem has never stopped loving us. And not only as a nation — He loves each and every one of us dearly.

FASCINATING FACTS

From the time Yaakov and his family came down to Egypt until they left was 210 years.

From the time Hashem told Avraham that his children would be the Chosen People and that they would suffer in a foreign country until the Exodus (when the Jews left Egypt) was 430 years. From the time Yitzchak was born until the Exodus was 400 years.

is no food or water there. After everything they had seen Hashem do for them, they had absolute *emunah*, complete faith in Him. They knew they could follow Hashem anywhere — even into the desert — completely certain that He would take care of them. No need to bring anything.

At Last!

On Thursday, the first day of Pesach, the fifteenth day of Nissan, in the 2,448th year after Hashem created the world, the Jews were finally free.

We don't know all the details, but we can imagine that it looked something like this: millions of Jews, men, women, and children, as far as the eye could see. Just counting only the men between the ages of 20-60, there are 600,000. They are organized like twelve brigades of soldiers, forming twelve neat rows, a row for each of the twelve shevatim (tribes).

Fathers, mothers, and children are walking, together with their donkeys, who are loaded with wealth. They are heading to the Egyptian border. They are on the road to Sinai.

They are being led by Moshe Rabbeinu, walking tall and erect. With him is Yosef's coffin. Beside him is Aharon. Not far from them walks the woman who saved Moshe's life and raised him — Bisya, Pharaoh's daughter. Rising high above them is a sign of the Presence of Hashem for everyone to see: a cloud in the shape of a pillar that leads the way.

Behind them, as they leave Egypt, they can hear the cries of the Egyptians, "Move faster! Leave! Get out! Go! Go!" It was just as Moshe had said: The nation that had held the Jews in slavery was now begging them to leave.

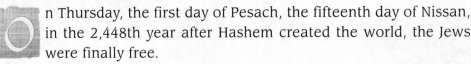

Pharaoh himself, and the most important people in the country, ride alongside them.

The Jews had come to Egypt as a family of seventy people. Now they were leaving Egypt — a nation of millions!

More Mitzvos

At the end of the parashah, Hashem gives us more mitzvos. These will help us remember the wonderful kindness and miracles Hashem did for us to get us out of Egypt. Here are some details about these mitzvos:

The Mitzvos of the Firstborn

T here are three mitzvos about the firstborn.

Pidyon Haben: The father of a firstborn boy gives five silver shekels to a Kohen when the child is thirty days old to redeem him.

Kiddush Bechor Beheimah: A firstborn male sheep, goat, or bull is holy and in the times of the Beis HaMikdash was given to a Kohen, who brought it as a korban.

If a firstborn animal has a blemish, it can't be used as a korban. It is given to the Kohen to eat.

Pidyon Petter Chamor: Of all the non-kosher animals, only the donkey has the honor of its firstborn male being holy. That's because the donkeys were so helpful to the Jews when they left Egypt. They were the ones that carried all the wealth on their backs.

The law is that when a firstborn male donkey is born it can't be used by the owner until it is redeemed with a sheep or goat, which is given to the Kohen.

Why is pidyon haben a relatively rare mitzvah?

Let's figure it out. About half of newborn babies are girls. Out of the half who are boys, only the mother's firstborn son has a pidyon haben, so if her firstborn is a girl, even if she has a boy later, there is no mitzvah. And if the father is a Kohen or Levi, or the mother is the daughter of a Kohen or Levi, her firstborn son also doesn't have a pidyon haben. So when a father makes a pidyon haben it's quite a celebration.

The Mitzvah of Tefillin

T efillin are a Jewish man's most precious possession. Jewish men can be seen wearing tefillin in airplanes, when they are in the army, or in a hospital. Jewish men put on tefillin every day, except for Shabbos or Yom Tov.

There is a famous question people sometimes ask themselves. Imagine that your house is burning down. There is no one inside, so no one is in danger. You can save only one thing. What would you save? For a Jewish man it's a no-brainer. He will save his tefillin.

(For more on the laws and customs of tefillin, see page 59.)

Haggadah

O n the anniversary of the night we were freed from Egypt, we have a mitzvah to tell in great detail and excitement the story of our slavery and the many miracles that Hashem did for us. We should talk about all the amazing stories: Moshe's incredible stick, the Makkos, the Jews leaving Egypt, Kriyas Yam Suf.

We should tell our children the whole story. And even if you are celebrating Pesach all alone, you should tell the story … to yourself.

To help us do this mitzvah our Rabbis wrote the Haggadah, which we all read and talk about at our Seder.

MORE ON THE MITZVOS
THE MITZVAH OF DECLARING ROSH CHODESH

Look Up!

 In the second half of a Jewish month, the moon gets smaller and smaller, until it disappears. Then we start to see it again, little by little.

For many, many years, people who saw the first sliver of the moon would travel to the great Jewish court, the Sanhedrin, and would tell the judges what they had seen.

The judges would ask questions. How high in the sky was the moon? How wide was it? Where in the sky was it? The judges had to make sure that these people really saw the moon.

Once the court heard from two witnesses who had seen the new moon, the head of the court would say, "Mekudash, holy." Then everyone else would answer, "Mekudash mekudash." That meant that the day was Rosh Chodesh, the first day of the new month. It was a day of celebration when Jews would recite Hallel and an extra Shemoneh Esrei called Mussaf. In the Beis HaMikdash there would be special korbanos.

Torches

 How did the court let the whole country know that it was Rosh Chodesh?

They lit torches!

Once the Sanhedrin declared the new month, they sent someone to light a torch on the top of Har HaZeisim, the Mount of Olives, in Yerushalayim. On a faraway mountaintop, a Jew was waiting for that signal. When he saw the torch, he lit his own torch. When the person on the next mountain saw that, he lit his. In a short time, the news that it was Rosh Chodesh reached everyone.

FASCINATING FACTS

In the year 4121 from Creation (361 CE), it looked like the Romans would make it impossible for a court to proclaim Rosh Chodesh. The leader of the last court in Eretz Yisrael was Hillel II. He and his judges calculated when the first day of each month should be for all the years to come. They made all those future first days of the month Rosh Chodesh.

For over 1650 years we've been using the same calendar that they made!

THE MITZVAH OF KORBAN PESACH
YOU ARE THERE

Imagine what it was like in Yerushalayim on Erev Pesach two thousand years ago. Millions of Jews are coming from all directions, walking up the mountain to the Beis HaMikdash. A solid column of smoke rises from the Mizbei'ach (Altar). Jews are either leading or holding young lambs or goats in their arms.

You and your family join them and take your animal to the Beis HaMikdash. You find yourself standing in front of a high gate whose massive doors are closed. The first group has already come in and are now bringing their korban.

The doors open. The first group leaves and your group enters. When the Courtyard is full you hear the sounds of shofars, and behind you the doors close. Then the most beautiful music you have ever heard begins. It's coming from a platform where Levi'im are playing instruments and singing Hallel. Around the Mizbei'ach are rows and rows of Kohanim.

You get in line, and after your animal is slaughtered and the avodah (service) completed, you take it to where you are staying in Yerushalayim. There you put the entire uncut meat of the lamb on a stick and roast it over a fire.

At the Seder, you will eat matzah and maror, and everyone in your group will end the meal with a piece of the Korban Pesach. Hillel's custom was to make a sandwich of the maror, matzah, and meat from the Korban Pesach, eating everything together at once. Today, we make a sandwich of matzah and maror.

When Mashiach Comes

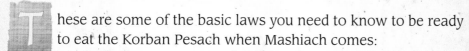

These are some of the basic laws you need to know to be ready to eat the Korban Pesach when Mashiach comes:

▸ The Korban Pesach is brought from a lamb or goat that is less than one year old.
▸ A Jewish man who has no bris can't bring the korban or eat from it.
▸ A father whose son is over eight days old can't eat from the korban unless his son has a bris.
▸ You can't give the meat to a non-Jew to eat.
▸ The animal is roasted whole over a fire on a spit.
▸ When eating it you can't break any of its bones.
▸ It can't be taken outside the walls of Yerushalayim.
▸ The entire korban should be eaten by midnight.
▸ Any leftovers are burned on the first day of Chol HaMoed.

THE MITZVOS OF PESACH

No Chametz

Flour that has been in contact with water for more than 18 minutes without being worked on is chametz.

The night before the Seder we do bedikas chametz by the light of a candle, making sure our rooms, closets, and games are chametz-free.

In the morning we burn the chametz.

From mid-morning of Erev Pesach until Pesach is over, chametz may not be eaten.

From before noontime of Erev Pesach until Pesach is over we are not allowed to even own chametz. That is why we burn our chametz before that time. When that time has passed you can't give it to your animals to eat and you can't sell it either.

The Richest Man

One of the ways we make sure not to own chametz is to sell it to a non-Jew and then buy it back from him after Pesach.

After the sale, a non-Jew who buys the chametz of a large Jewish bakery is very wealthy — but he also owes the owners the money for buying the company. But after Pesach he sells it all back, and he no longer owes the money.

Eat Matzah

A person should eat the proper amount of matzah on the Seder night. One can ask his Rabbi how much that is, or there are guides and charts that show the size.

Matzah reminds us of the slavery in Egypt because the Jews used to eat matzah when they were slaves.

It also reminds us that when we left Egypt we left in such a hurry that the dough didn't have a chance to rise and become chametz.

Making Matzah

Matzah is made only of flour and water. It has to be made very quickly — in less than 18 minutes. If it is left untouched for more than 18 minutes it becomes chametz.

We can't use just any matzah for the mitzvah at the Seder. The matzah had to have been made for the purpose of doing the mitzvah of eating matzah. The people who work on making the matzah say out loud, "for the purpose of the mitzvah of

QUESTIONS, ANYONE?

How hot is the oven the matzah is baked in? 1000 degrees for the hand matzah; 800 degrees for the machine matzah.

How long does it take to bake a matzah? About 30-40 seconds for a hand matzah; one minute 20 seconds for a machine matzah.

matzah." It is best to use matzah made from grain that was guarded from becoming chametz from the time it was cut on the farm. This matzah is called "shemurah mishaas ketzirah," guarded from the time of cutting.

THE MITZVAH OF TEFILLIN

How Tefillin Boxes Are Made

Ever wonder what tefillin boxes are made of? Or how they have such a perfectly square shape?

The person making the batim (boxes) starts with a thick piece of animal hide. Nowadays, it usually comes from a bull. This is pressed over square metal blocks in a hydraulic press. The great pressure squeezes the animal hide into a perfectly square box. For hand-tefillin (tefillin shel yad) the box has one large space in the center, while head-tefillin (tefillin shel rosh) has four separate spaces.

The box for the head has a "four-headed" shin on one side and a "three-headed" shin on the other. This is done by molding the hide by hand, something like what you do when shaping clay.

What's Inside?

Inside the boxes are Torah portions written by hand on parchment. They make the tefillin holy and kosher to wear. These parts of the Torah teach us to love Hashem, to believe that He runs the world, to accept His mitzvos, and to remember that He took the Jews out of Egypt.

The hand-tefillin contains a long piece of parchment which has written on it four parts from the Torah arranged in four columns. The first and the second come from the end of Parashas Bo. They discuss leaving Egypt, the mitzvah of pidyon haben, and the command to put on tefillin.

The third part is Shema Yisrael and the first paragraph of Shema, "V'ahavta," which is about believing in Hashem, loving Him, and wearing tefillin and putting mezuzos on our doorposts.

The fourth column is the next part of Shema — "V'hayah im shamoa." This teaches us to listen to Hashem's mitzvos and to wear tefillin and put up mezuzos.

The head-tefillin contains the same parts of the Torah, also written on parchment. But instead of one long piece, each part is written on a separate parchment, and they are inserted into the four sections.

QUESTIONS, ANYONE?

Why does one shin on the head-tefillin have four heads and the other three?

Three reminds us of the fathers of the Jewish people: Avraham, Yitzchak, and Yaakov.

The four-headed shin is for the mothers of the Jewish people: Sarah, Rivkah, Rachel, and Leah.

פָּרָשַׁת בְּשַׁלַּח

Parashas Beshalach

Beshalach · בְּשַׁלַּח

Parashah Pointers

▸ The Jews leave Egypt, carrying Yosef's coffin, surrounded by the Ananei HaKavod (Clouds of Glory). They are guided by a cloud-shaped pillar by day and a pillar of fire by night.

▸ Hashem takes them the long way to Eretz Yisrael, through the desert, so that it would be hard for them to go back to Egypt.

▸ After the Jews travel for two days, Hashem tells them to turn back toward Egypt.

▸ Pharaoh decides to chase after the Jews with a large army. When the Jews see Pharaoh's army coming at them they panic. Moshe assures them that Hashem will save them.

▸ Hashem has Moshe split the sea and the Jews go in. The Egyptians follow them.

▸ After the Jews are safely out of the sea, the waters come crashing down on the Egyptian army, drowning them.

▸ The Jews sing a song of thanks to Hashem.

▸ The sea spits out the Egyptian bodies, and the gold, silver, and jewelry the Egyptians had taken with them. The Jews pick up a fortune from the beach.

▸ The Jews travel to Marah, where the water is bitter. They complain to Moshe that they need water. Hashem tells Moshe to throw a piece of bitter wood into the water. Miraculously, the bitter water becomes sweet.

▸ At Marah they are taught some of the Torah's laws.

▸ They travel to Eilim, where they find date trees and springs of water.

▸ A month after leaving Egypt they arrive at Midbar Sinn (Sinn Desert). They complain to Moshe that they have no food. Hashem sends them heavenly food, called mahn (manna). He also sends them birds to eat.

▸ Even though the Jews were told that the mahn would not fall on Shabbos, some of them go to look for it anyway.

▸ The Jews come to Refidim, and again there is no water. They complain to Moshe. Hashem tells Moshe to take his stick and hit a rock. A miracle happens and water comes pouring out of the rock.

▸ The nation of Amalek attacks the Jews for no reason. Yehoshua leads the battle against them while Moshe prays for them. The Jews win. Hashem gives the command that Amalek must be wiped off the face of the earth.

No Questions Asked

he Jews, now free, marched out into the desert. They were surrounded by the Ananei HaKavod. These clouds surrounded them, protecting them from the desert sun and the heat.

In front of them was a cloud shaped like a pillar, rising high to the sky. It showed the Jews where to go. Wherever the cloud went, they followed.

The Jews were amazing! Imagine going on a long trip and never asking, "Where are we going? How long will it take to get there? Are we there yet? What will we eat and drink in the desert?" The Jews just followed wherever Hashem led them, no questions asked by any of the three million travelers! They all had perfect faith and trust in Hashem.

Even today, Hashem always remembers the outstanding faith and trust of His three million children — Bnei Yisrael — at that time.

Pillar of Fire

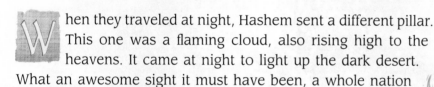hen they traveled at night, Hashem sent a different pillar. This one was a flaming cloud, also rising high to the heavens. It came at night to light up the dark desert. What an awesome sight it must have been, a whole nation traveling by the intense light of a fiery pillar.

The cloud traveling in front of them killed snakes and scorpions that could hurt the Jews. Hashem wanted their journey to be easy, so the cloud would also flatten the hills and fill any holes in the desert.

Yosef and Pharaoh

hen the Jews left Egypt, Pharaoh himself escorted them part of the way. On the way out of Egypt, Moshe took Yosef's coffin. (To read how Moshe found Yosef's body, see page 53 in Parashas Bo.)

The Long Way

If you wanted to go from New York City to Miami, you wouldn't drive west to Chicago and then go southeast to Miami. You would drive south, along the Atlantic Ocean. That's a direct route and gets you there much more quickly.

When the Jews left Egypt they were on the way to Eretz Yisrael. The shortest way to get there from Egypt would be to go in a straight path along the coast of the Mediterranean Sea. Instead, Hashem told them to go into the desert, which is the long way to get to Eretz Yisrael. Why?

FASCINATING FACTS

The pillars of cloud and of fire were symbols of Hashem's Presence. They showed that Hashem Himself was escorting us as we traveled. Why did we deserve to have Hashem as our personal escort?

It was because of Avraham Avinu. Though Avraham was a wealthy man with many servants, he himself personally escorted his three visitors on their way when they had finished their meal.

The visitors were angels. They had come to tell Avraham the good news that he and Sarah would have a son, and to heal him from the pain of his bris.

When the visitors left, Abraham escorted them. What was his reward? Hashem escorted Avraham's grandchildren when they left Egypt.

TORAH in our LIVES

The Torah says that the Jews left Egypt "chamushim" — armed.* You may ask, after they had seen how Hashem had done so many miracles for them, why did they think they needed weapons? Wouldn't Hashem protect them?

From this we can learn that we are not allowed to rely on a miracle. We can't sit around all day and say: "Hashem will make a miracle to help us."

We do what has to be done to succeed without miracles. For tests — we study. To protect ourselves — we wear a helmet. To get well — we go to doctors. At the same time, we know that if we do well or we are saved — it was Hashem's doing.

_____

*There is another opinion that the word "chamushim" does not mean "armed." Instead, the Torah is telling us that only one out of every five Jews (five in Hebrew is "chamesh") left Egypt (Rashi). To find out what happened to the other 4/5, see page 44 in Parashas Bo.

To answer that question you have to know what happened when some Jews escaped Egypt before Yetzias Mitzrayim.

Escape

Yignon was a man from Shevet Ephraim. Thirty years before the Jews left Egypt, he convinced others in his shevet that the time had come to leave Egypt. Unfortunately, he was wrong! He and thousands of his followers fought their way out of Egypt and escaped.

After leaving Egypt there was only one place they wanted to go: Eretz Yisrael, the land Hashem promised to give the Jewish people. Taking the fastest route from Egypt to Eretz Yisrael, they traveled along the Mediterranean coast.

Tragedy

Then, tragedy struck! On their way to Eretz Yisrael, these Jews were attacked. All of them were killed, and their bodies were left unburied.

Now the time had really come to leave Egypt. The Jews were finally free! If they would have taken the quick way to Eretz Yisrael, they would have seen the bones of Ephraim's shevet scattered over the fields. Many Jews would be frightened, and they would want to run back to Egypt. That's why Hashem took them the long way.

Other Reasons

There are many other reasons that Hashem took them the long way. Here are some:

Hashem wanted them to get the Torah at Har Sinai, which was in the desert.

On the short route to Eretz Yisrael, there were many people who might attack them. If that would happen, the Jews might get scared and return to Egypt. But if Hashem took them the long way, it would be much harder for them to go back to Egypt.

The Trip Continues

On the day the Jews left Egypt, the fifteenth of Nissan (the first day of Pesach), they went from Ramses to Succos. The next day they traveled from Succos to Eisam. On the third day a big fight broke out!

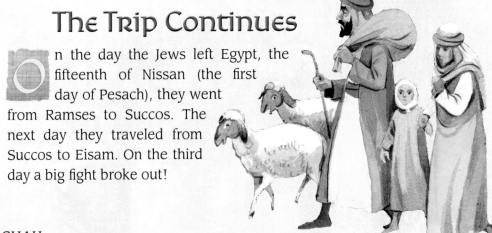

Get Back to Work

Pharaoh had sent his officers to follow the Jews and see what would happen to them. At the end of the three days, these officers saw that the Jews were not packing up and returning to Egypt. They got very angry. "Why are you just hanging around? You asked Pharaoh to let you go for three days to serve Hashem. Now the three days are up. Get back to work!"

Fight!

What are you talking about?" the Jews answered them. "On the night of the tenth makkah, Pharaoh walked around our neighborhoods and announced that we are free. We aren't going back. Never!"

A big fight broke out. Some of the Egyptians were killed, and others barely escaped. Those who survived ran back to Egypt and reported to Pharaoh.

And then something very surprising happened.

Freedom Valley

Until now the Jews were traveling **away** from Egypt. Now Moshe commanded them to do an about-face. The Jews found themselves **returning** to Egypt! They traveled from Eisam to Pi Hachiros. This was a city near the Egyptian border. It had been called Pisom, and it was one of the cities that the Egyptians had forced their Jewish slaves to build. They camped right by an enormous stone idol called Baal-Tzefon.

One More Chance

Why was Hashem bringing the Jews back to Egypt? And why was Baal-Tzefon not destroyed during Makkas Bechoros, like all the other Egyptian idols?

This was all part of Hashem's plan. He wasn't quite finished with Pharaoh and Egypt yet. Once again, Pharaoh would be given the chance to choose between good and evil.

To give Pharaoh that choice, Hashem didn't destroy Baal-Tzefon. When Pharaoh would hear that the Jews were near Baal-Tzefon, would he think that his idol was more powerful than Hashem? Had he learned his lesson of the Ten Makkos — that Hashem is the greatest power in the world? Or did he still believe in his own idols?

Would he let the Jews stay free, or would he try to enslave them again?

How did the Egyptians still have horses after all the makkos?

Makkas Dever killed only the animals "in the field," and that was true by Barad as well. The Egyptians who feared Hashem brought their animals inside by Barad. These G-d-fearing Egyptians weren't very G-d fearing; they now gave their horses to chase the Jews.

FASCINATING FACTS

Though there wasn't much distance between the Egyptians and the Jews, Pharaoh's army never got close enough to do the Jews any harm.

The cloud-shaped pillar moved in front of the Egyptian army, separating them from the Jews. All the Egyptians' arrows fell into the cloud, doing no damage.

Now's My Chance!

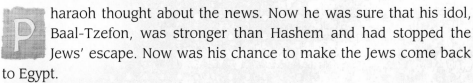

Pharaoh thought about the news. Now he was sure that his idol, Baal-Tzefon, was stronger than Hashem and had stopped the Jews' escape. Now was his chance to make the Jews come back to Egypt.

He told his ministers, "What have we done? Why did we send away our slaves? Think of all the money we lost by freeing hundreds of thousands of slaves who worked for free. What about all our treasures they escaped with? Each one had ninety donkey loads of gold and silver. Are we going to let them go?"

Pharaoh's servants said, "NO! You are right! Let's get them back."

In their greed they forgot their suffering by Hashem's hand during the Makkos.

Take What You Want!

But when Pharaoh told his soldiers about his plans to bring the Jews back, they didn't want to join him. They still remembered how much they had suffered from the Makkos. They were afraid to fight the Jews.

Pharaoh knew how to change their minds. He said, "I usually keep what my army captures from my enemies, but this time I will share it with all of you! Think how rich you will be! Imagine all the wealth we will take back from the Jews when we catch them! Also, whoever joins me to bring the Jews back can take what he wants from my treasure."

The soldiers forgot their fears and joined Pharaoh. 200,000 foot soldiers, 50,000 men on horses,* and all the chariots in Egypt were ready to chase after the Jews.

Tanks and Chariots

In those ancient days the chariots were like today's tanks. They were very powerful fighting machines. Along with a huge army, Pharaoh organized 600 of the best horse-drawn chariots in all of Egypt.

Normally a Pharaoh (Egyptian king) did not go out to the battlefield. But this time he personally tied his horses to the royal chariot and rode out to chase the Jews, leading his men into battle.

Some opinions say there were even more!

Fear and Terror

On the night of the twenty-first of Nissan the Jews saw the Egyptian soldiers coming at them. Even more terrifying, Hashem let them see the terrifying heavenly angel of Egypt flying over the army.

There was fear and terror in the Jewish camp. Fathers and mothers worried about their lives and the lives of their children. People looked around for a place to run. To escape.

Trapped!

The way to the desert was blocked by wild, howling animals. In front of them was the sea, behind them the Egyptian army. They were trapped. There was nowhere to go. Nowhere to run.

There was only one thing to do. And they did it. They prayed to Hashem.

The Argument

There were Jews who yelled at Moshe. "Aren't there enough graves in Egypt?" they said. "Why did you take us out here to die? Why did you take us out of Egypt?"

QUESTIONS, ANYONE?

The Egyptians are getting closer and closer and Hashem tells Moshe to **stop praying?** Why?

One answer is: Hashem told him to stop praying because the Jews had already prayed for themselves, and because of those prayers He would save them! Moshe's prayers to save them were no longer necessary.

Another answer: Moshe had been praying for a long time. Hashem told him, "Now is not the time for long prayers, it is the time for action." He then told Moshe what must be done to save the Jews.

Why didn't Hashem tell Moshe to use his stick to split the sea?

Hashem didn't want the Egyptians to think that Moshe's miracles happened because his stick had great powers. So at Kriyas Yam Suf Hashem told Moshe to do this miracle without the stick, just by stretching his hand over the water.

Now everyone saw that Moshe himself performed the miracles, it wasn't his stick.

FASCINATING FACTS

When the waters of the sea split, so did all the waters all over the world.

WHO'S WHO IN THE TORAH

Nachshon ben Aminadav

- Aharon married Nachshon's sister Elisheva, making them brothers-in-law.
- Nachshon was the leader of Shevet Yehudah.
- His descendants included many great heroes, including King David and the future Mashiach.

The Jews began to argue about what to do. They came to Moshe with their opinions.

Some said, "We would rather die than go back to Egypt. We're going to jump into the sea and drown ourselves."

Moshe said, "Don't do it. Hashem will save you."

Others said, "Let's fight our enemies!"

Moshe told them, "Hashem will fight for you."

Some said, "We have to surrender and return to Egypt as slaves." Moshe said, "Don't worry, this is the last time you will see the Egyptians."

Go!

Meanwhile, the Egyptians were getting closer and closer. Moshe began to pray.

Hashem spoke to Moshe and said, "Why are you crying out to Me? Tell the Jews to go forward! Stretch your hand over the sea. It will split and the Jews will walk through on dry land."

Moshe told his people to go forward into the sea.

To Go or Not to Go?

The Jews were scared. Not just scared — terrified! To go into the sea or not to go? To trust Moshe or to trust your eyes, which see nothing but a raging sea in front of you? Not an easy decision.

One Man of Faith

No tribe wanted to be the first to go into the water. Suddenly, the people saw one man jump in. When he heard Moshe's command, he jumped into the sea, with absolute faith in Hashem and Moshe — no questions asked.

His name was Nachshon ben Aminadav. He was the Nasi, prince, of Shevet Yehudah.

The Jews on the beach watched Nachshon as he walked further and further into the water. It was already up to his waist. The water had not split!

He didn't stop. The water was up to his shoulders already. Still no miracle. Now he was up to his nose in the water. Any further and he would drown.

And finally, at the very last moment — the sea split!

When did the sea split?

The Jews left Egypt on the 15th of Nissan, which became the first day of Pesach. They crossed the sea on the night of the 21st of Nissan, the seventh day of Pesach. To make sure that we remember these two great miracles, the Torah says that the first day and seventh day of Pesach are special holidays, when most work is forbidden. Later, the Rabbis added the second and eighth days of Pesach as Yamim Tovim, holidays, for Jews living outside of Eretz Yisrael. The days between those holidays are Chol HaMoed, when certain types of work are allowed.

FASCINATING FACTS

Even the simplest Jews at Kriyas Yam Suf were so holy that they saw a very clear vision of how Hashem runs the world. They even saw more than some of the greatest prophets.

Kriyas Yam Suf / The Splitting of the Sea

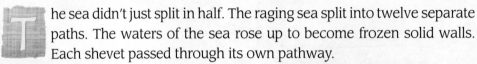

As all the Jews watched, the greatest miracle they had ever seen happened before their eyes. The waters of the sea split! With the Egyptian army chasing after them, wanting to capture or kill them, the Jews raced into the sea, which then became dry land!

Many, many miracles happened on that night. Let's remember some of them.

Twelve Roads

The sea didn't just split in half. The raging sea split into twelve separate paths. The waters of the sea rose up to become frozen solid walls. Each shevet passed through its own pathway.

As the Jews walked on their roads, Hashem made roofs over them. They didn't have to step into the wet mud of the sea bed. Instead, there was a dry floor under their feet. Not only was it dry, it was beautiful, since it dried like floor tiles. And Hashem made a roof over their heads.

The walls were see-through. That way people could see their friends and relatives from different shevatim, walking safely across what had been the sea.

Water Fountains and Fruit Trees

Imagine: The Jews are walking through the dried sea, and a little child starts to cry. He's thirsty! His mother touches the wall — and out comes sweet water. And what about food? There's plenty to eat. The Jews walking through the tunnels see fruit trees miraculously growing out of the ground. There's even some grass growing for the animals to munch on.

Punishment

Though the Jews had escaped Pharaoh's army, they were still not out of danger. Pharaoh and his chariots were racing after them across the dry sea bed, still trying to catch them!

Now the time had come for the Egyptians to be punished for throwing newborn Jewish baby boys into the river. Pharaoh and his advisers had chosen to kill the babies with water. They thought Hashem couldn't punish them with water because He had promised Noach not to bring another flood on the world.

But the Egyptians were mistaken. First, Hashem only promised not to flood the entire world. Second, instead of bringing water to flood Egypt, Hashem would bring the Egyptians to the water, where they would drown.

Horses, Chariots, and Soldiers

Hashem destroyed the enemies of the Jews in a miraculous way.

When Pharaoh's army saw the sea split they didn't turn around and run away in fright at seeing such a strange sight. Instead, they followed the Jews into the sea, as if the sea splitting were a normal thing. After all, doesn't it happen every day?

That was a miracle. And there were more miracles to come.

The pillar-shaped cloud touched the dry sea floor that the Jews had walked over, and turned it into mud. Then the pillar of fire touched the mud — and it began to boil!

When the Egyptian forces came charging into the sea, the horses and heavy chariots sank into the sea floor, and the boiling mud burned off the chariot wheels.

The horses kept racing forward without chariot wheels. The Egyptians' bones broke from the bumpy ride.

To frighten the soldiers, Hashem filled the air with a constant booming of great claps of thunder.

FASCINATING FACTS

When Moshe stretched his hand over the sea, the sea didn't want to split. The angel in charge of the sea told Moshe, "You can't order me around. Humans were created on Friday, the last day of Creation. I was created before you, on Tuesday, the third day of Creation. I am greater than you."

Moshe told Hashem what the angel said. Hashem then rested His Presence on Moshe's hand. When the sea saw that, it split.

Others say that the angel saw Yosef's coffin being carried out of Egypt. Because of Yosef's great mitzvah of running away from Potiphar's wife, the sea agreed to split.

The End

It was in the middle of the night, a few hours before dawn. All the Jews were safely out of the sea and on the beach. All the Egyptians were in the middle of the sea. Hashem called to Moshe, "Stretch your arm over the sea and the water will go back to the way it was before it split."

The Jews watched as Moshe held his arm out over the sea. Suddenly the solid walls of the sea melted and the water came crashing down on their enemies.

Swallowed

When the solid sea walls came crashing down on their heads the Egyptians were swallowed by the water. Hashem sent strong waves to lift the chariots and their drivers into the air. The chariots overturned, spilling their drivers and soldiers into the water.

Some of Pharaoh's soldiers suffered very much. Hashem had the waves toss them into the air again and again so that they drowned slowly and painfully. This happened to those Egyptians who had been most cruel to the Jews.

The average Egyptians sank slowly, like a rock sinking into water. Those who were not so cruel to their Jewish slaves sank into the sea like heavy pieces of lead. They drowned quickly, with less pain.

FASCINATING FACTS

When the Egyptians were drowning, the angels in heaven wanted to sing praise to Hashem. But Hashem wouldn't let them. He said, "The people I created are drowning in the sea, and you want to sing?"

It was all right for the Jews to sing. They were singing a song to thank Hashem for saving them.

We Believe!

After the Egyptians had drowned, Hashem had the sea spit out their bodies onto the beach. Seeing their dead enemies, the Jews knew their slavery was really over. They were finally free of their Egyptian masters, forever!

After they saw everything that happened, the Jews were in awe of Hashem. Now they truly believed with their whole hearts that Hashem was all-powerful, and that He had sent Moshe to save them.

Az Yashir: The Song at the Sea

Moshe and the Jews were so happy they were saved that they broke out in heavenly-inspired song. This song is so important that we say it *every single day* in our morning prayers.

All Together

Moshe would sing one line of the song and the Jews joyously sang together, repeating Moshe's words. He led them, and all of the Jews sang the song together perfectly, as if they had practiced it many times. They all started at the same time and ended at the same time. Imagine the beauty and power of all those voices singing praises to Hashem!

Praise and Thanks

hat did the Jews sing about?

They praised and thanked Hashem for:

▸ The miracles that happened at Kriyas Yam Suf. They described in detail how they had been saved.

▸ Hashem's power — there is no one like Him.

▸ The respect and fear that Edom and the other nations had for the Jews when they heard about the miraculous destruction of the Egyptian army.

The Future

hey also sang about what would happen in the future.

▸ The miracles that will happen when Mashiach comes will be greater than the ones that happened at Yetzias Mitzrayim.

▸ All nations will accept Hashem as King and Ruler of the world.

▸ There will be a third Beis HaMikdash that will come down from Heaven and that will last forever.

The Jews' Commitment

n the Song at the Sea the Jews promised not only to do the mitzvos, but to do them in a beautiful way. That's why we decorate the succah, buy a nice esrog and beautiful tefillin, have lovely things on our Shabbos table, and so on.

Gold and Drums?

hen the Jewish men left Egypt they took all the wealth of Egypt, packing gold and silver and jewels.

And the women? They also packed drums.

Now why would they do that? Why would the women insist on packing drums?

Because they had faith. They were sure that Hashem would make great miracles for them, and that they would want to celebrate with song. To help them celebrate, they took drums.

TORAH in our LIVES

The Jews were right to ask for water. Without water, who can live? But the way they asked for it was wrong. After everything Hashem and Moshe had done for them, why did they get angry and complain? They should have been polite and asked Moshe, "Please pray to Hashem to give us water."

Sometimes there is something we want and need. A new bike, basketball, or a popular game. It's okay to ask for it. But make sure you ask your parents politely.

QUESTIONS, ANYONE?

Why didn't Hashem make the water sweet before they arrived at Marah?

The Jews didn't want to leave the sea shore to receive the Torah because of the wealth they were picking off the beach. Hashem wanted to teach the Jews that money isn't everything. So He made sure that when they got to Marah they would find bitter water instead of drinkable water. They had a lot of money, but you can't drink or eat money.

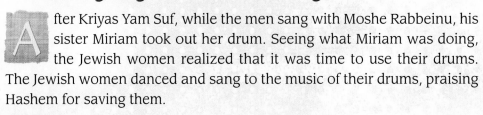

Singing and Dancing

After Kriyas Yam Suf, while the men sang with Moshe Rabbeinu, his sister Miriam took out her drum. Seeing what Miriam was doing, the Jewish women realized that it was time to use their drums. The Jewish women danced and sang to the music of their drums, praising Hashem for saving them.

Treasure on the Beach

Imagine you are at the beach. A wave washes onto the sand, and when it goes back to the sea you see it has left a wooden treasure chest full of gold. Another wave comes by, bringing a diamond necklace. How long would you stay there in the hope that the next waves would bring you more great things?

That's what happened to the Jews. The Egyptian chariots and horses were decorated with all kinds of gold, silver, and jewelry. And Hashem had the sea throw it on the beach for the Jews to pick up.

The Jews stayed on the beach, hoping more and more treasure would come up. They didn't want to leave. Maybe there would be more?

Finally, Moshe forced them to follow him and they left the sea, traveling through the Shur Desert.

Bitter Water

The Jews traveled in the desert for three days and reached a place called Marah. By now they had run out of water. In Marah they found water. They filled their cups and began to drink. But then they spit it out, because the water was bitter, undrinkable. Desperate and thirsty, they complained to Moshe, "What will we drink!?"

Hashem showed Moshe a tree whose wood is bitter and told him to throw it into the water. All the Jews watched as Moshe threw the bitter-tasting wood into the water. A miracle happened and the water became sweet.

Taste of Torah

While they were at Marah, Hashem gave them a "taste" of Torah. He gave them some mitzvos there, including the mitzvos of Shabbos, honoring parents, and Parah Adumah (the Red Cow). He also gave them the laws of how courts should judge cases between people who disagree about money matters.

70 and 12

T he Jews' next stop was Eilim. It was an oasis in the desert. When He made the world, Hashem prepared 12 springs of water in this place, in honor of the twelve shevatim. There were also 70 palm trees full of luscious dates. Why 70? To honor the 70 great wise men who were leaders of the Jewish people.

While they rested in that pleasant place, the Jews learned the parts of the Torah they were given in Marah.

It was time to move on. The next stop: Midbar Sinn — the Sinn Desert. They got there on the fifteenth of Iyar, a month after they had left Egypt.

Food?

F or all the days the Jews had traveled since leaving Egypt they had been eating the matzos that they took with them.

And here was still another miracle: No matter how many times they reached into their bags to eat, there was always more to eat the next day!

When they arrived at Midbar Sinn they still had matzah — but when they reached into their bags after eating, there was nothing left! They turned the bags upside down and shook them. Nothing was left, not even a crumb.

Panic!

T he Jews panicked. Where would they find enough food to feed hundreds of thousands of Jewish families for the next day? They would starve!

They came to Moshe and Aharon and complained, "It would have been better to die in Egypt where we had bread and meat. Why did you take us out here to the desert to die horribly of starvation?!!"

Saved!

M oshe told the Jews, "Why are you complaining against us? You're really complaining against Hashem. He's the one Who gives food. He has heard your complaints. This afternoon you will eat meat, and in the morning food will come down from heaven."

That afternoon an enormous flock of fat juicy birds came flying down over the camp. They were in easy reach of the Jews. The people would just stick their hands out and catch as many birds as they wanted to eat.

FASCINATING FACTS

Hashem promised the Jews that if they obey His laws and mitzvos, and deal honestly in business, they will not get ill. There is no greater doctor than Hashem, Who knows what's good for the body.

What is good for the body? The Torah and mitzvos that Hashem gave us.

What does the word mahn mean?

When the Jews first saw the mahn they asked "mahn hu? — what is it?" And that's why it's called mahn.

Another answer: What do you call something you eat? Food. Mahn means prepared food.

What blessing did the Jews make on the mahn?

They couldn't say, "hamotzi lechem min **haaretz** — Who supplies bread from the **earth**," because the mahn came from heaven. The Jews said, "hamotzi lechem min **hashamayim** — Who supplies bread from the **heavens**."

TORAH IN OUR LIVES

We do something special every Shabbos to remember the miracle of the mahn. The two challahs on our Shabbos table remind us that on Friday twice as much mahn fell than it did on a regular weekday. We cover the challah on top and on bottom, reminding us of the layers of dew that were both under and over the mahn.

Everyone went to sleep satisfied and looking forward to the next morning, when Hashem had promised that food would rain down from heaven.

But What Is It?

The next morning the Jews got up and saw that the entire camp was surrounded by a layer of dew. As the sun got hotter the dew disappeared, to reveal miles and miles of what looked like white seeds resting on dew. No one had ever seen anything like it before.

"What is it?" everyone asked.

Moshe told them this was the food that Hashem sent from heaven.

Since no one knew what it was, they decided to call it mahn. They tasted the mahn, and it tasted like a honey-fried donut.

The Rules of the Mahn

Hashem wanted to test the Jews to see if they would obey His commandments, so along with the mahn came rules on how to use it.

▸ Every morning they should collect the mahn. But they should only pick up enough for one day. That was an omer (about 3⅔ quarts) of mahn for each person in the family.

▸ No mahn may be saved for the next day.

The Test

These rules were a hard test for the Jews. Imagine going to sleep at night with an empty fridge, and you have no idea if you will have food tomorrow. Wouldn't you save a little something under your pillow to be sure you have something to eat tomorrow?

This was Hashem's test. Would the Jews have the faith that Hashem would send food the next day?

Worms and Bad Smells

There were two wicked Jews, Dassan and Aviram. They were the two Jews whom Moshe had stopped from fighting each other in Egypt. And they were the ones who told Pharaoh that Moshe had killed an Egyptian.

Dassan and Aviram decided to disobey Hashem's command. They put away some of their mahn for the next day.

The next morning when they went to eat their leftover mahn for breakfast, they found it crawling with worms! And it smelled terrible.

Shabbos

The first day the mahn fell was a Sunday. Every day from Sunday to Thursday, the Jews collected an omer of mahn for each person. On Friday, though, when they got back from collecting the mahn, they found that they had two omers of mahn instead of just one!

The nesi'im (princes) of the shevatim went to Moshe to ask what was going on. Moshe explained that the next day was Shabbos, a holy day on which the mahn would not fall. Instead, everyone got a double portion on Friday, one portion for Friday and one for Shabbos. The extra portion would not rot, he said, and they would be able to eat it on Shabbos.

Birds

It is said that Dassan and Aviram wanted to show that Moshe was a liar. So they secretly put some mahn on the ground early Shabbos morning. They were hoping to fool the Jews into believing it had fallen on Shabbos, even though Moshe said no mahn would fall that day.

Some Jews couldn't resist. Even though Moshe had told them the mahn wouldn't fall, they went out to look anyway, "just to make sure." They went out and — just as Moshe had said — there was no mahn to be found!

What happened to the mahn that Dassan and Aviram had left on the ground? Birds flew down and ate it before the Jews got there.

Hashem was angry at the Jews for going out to collect mahn on Shabbos. He told Moshe, "Ask the Jews, 'How long will you refuse to do My commandments? On Shabbos, stay home and don't try to collect mahn.' "

FASCINATING FACTS

The Jews were traveling in the desert with three incredible gifts:

- food from heaven, called mahn
- water coming from a rock
- The Ananei HaKavod that surrounded them and protected them from desert heat and dangers

These gifts were given to us because of the good deeds of three righteous people:

- Moshe's merit brought the mahn.
- Aharon's merit brought the Ananei HaKavod.
- Miriam's merit brought the water.

Mahn's Special Miracles

▶ The unused mahn would melt, making streams that were drunk by deer. When non-Jews hunted the deer and ate them they enjoyed the heavenly taste of the mahn. It made them realize how great the Jews were that Hashem gave them such special food.

▶ No matter how much mahn someone put in his basket, when he came home there was always exactly an omer for each person in the family.

▶ The mahn tasted like a honey-roasted donut. But if someone wanted, it would taste like whatever he wanted: barbecued rib steak, fresh fruit, even candy!

▶ The mahn came down from heaven to feed the Jews in the desert for almost 40 years.

▶ After Moshe died on the seventh of Adar forty years later, the mahn stopped coming down. But miraculously, the mahn they had from the seventh of Adar lasted about five weeks, until they were able to make regular food in Eretz Yisrael.

▶ Hashem wrapped the mahn like a gift in a package. A layer of dew fell on the ground, then came the mahn, and finally it was covered by a layer of dew.

▶ Moshe told Aharon to take a jar of mahn and put it next to the Aron in the Mishkan's Kodesh HaKodashim (Holy of Holies). When the Beis HaMikdash was built, the jar was put in the Kodesh HaKodashim there.

▶ Before the destruction of the Beis HaMikdash, the jar and the Aron were hidden in a secret place. No one knows where they are. The jar is still there — and after all these years the mahn still has not spoiled.

FASCINATING FACTS

Chorev is another name for Har Sinai. The Jews continued drinking from this source of water for many years. The rock traveled with them through the desert. The rock was called Miriam's Well.

Whatever happened to Miriam's Well? Jewish tradition says that the Well of Miriam is hidden in the Kinneret (the Sea of Galilee).

More Complaints

The Jews left Midbar Sinn and traveled to Refidim. Again, they ran out of water. Again, they started to complain. They came to Moshe demanding that he give them water. Moshe prayed to Hashem and said, "What shall I do for this nation? Any minute now, they are going to throw stones at me."

Hashem told him, "Go to Har Chorev. Take the stick that you used to hit the Nile River. There I will show you a rock to hit with your stick. Water will flow from the rock. Since Har Chorev is far from Refidim, take some wise men of Israel with you. They will tell the Jews about the great miracle."

Moshe and the wise men went to Chorev. He hit the rock. Suddenly, water flowed from the rock. It flowed through the desert, all the way to where the Jews were camped. The Jews once again had water!

Testing and Arguing

Hashem knew what the Jews were thinking when they asked for water. Though they didn't say it, they thought to themselves: "Let's test Hashem. Is Hashem really with us or not? Will He give us water now?" They also argued with Moshe over the lack of water.

That's why the place where all this happened was called Massah (testing) U'Merivah (and arguing).

The War

Testing Hashem and arguing with Moshe was a big mistake. Now they were in trouble.

Out of nowhere, in the middle of the desert, came an army riding hard to attack the Jews. It was the nation of Amalek, descendants of Eisav!

The Jews had done nothing to Amalek. They had not attacked Amalek. The Amalekites were in no danger from the Jews whatsoever. Yet the Amalekites rode far out into the desert to try and destroy a people who had been slaves for so long and had finally become free.

Why did they attack innocent people for no reason? Because they hated the Jews and they hated Hashem. They were pure evil.

The poisonous hatred Amalek had for the Jews came from their ancestor Eisav, who hated his brother, Yaakov. Even more: Amalek hated the idea of an all-powerful G-d Who wants humans to be good. Amalek wanted to keep being evil.

The Jews Defend Themselves

Moshe told Yehoshua to put together an army and lead it to fight Amalek. He should accept only those men who were strong and who were the kind of people who were afraid to sin against Hashem. The battle would take place the next day.

Moshe understood that winning the war was not just about who has the most power and the best weapons — it was about whether the Jews would obey the Torah and trust Hashem. That is the best defense! Besides making sure that the soldiers were tzaddikim, Moshe also told the Jews that they should fast and do teshuvah on the day of the battle.

QUESTIONS, ANYONE?

Why did Hashem put the Jews in danger by letting Amalek attack them?

In Refidim, the Jews hadn't spent as much time learning the Torah they received at Marah as they should have. Whenever Jews don't devote enough time to Torah study, Amalek has power over them.

Another answer, which is a mashal (parable): A father is carrying his child on his shoulders. They pass a candy store. The child asks for a candy — and gets it. A bit later they pass a toy store. The child asks for a toy — and gets it. The same thing happens at the bakery.

As they are walking, the father meets one of his friends. The child looks down from on his father's shoulders and asks his father's friend, "Do you know where my daddy is?"

Hearing this, the father puts the child down. The child now has to walk on his own. On the way he gets bitten by a dog.

Here is the nimshal (the moral of the parable): Hashem had saved the Jews from so many dangers and given them so much! Yet at Refidim they had the nerve to ask, "Is Hashem with us or not?" So Hashem took away His protection and Amalek attacked. That would teach the Jews that Hashem had been with them all the time, and they should not test Him.

The Battle!

Yehoshua took his men out to fight Amalek. At the same time Moshe went up a mountain with his brother, Aharon, and their nephew Chur. He was the son of their sister, Miriam.

Standing on the mountain where the Jewish soldiers could see them, Moshe lifted his hands to pray to Hashem. When his hands were raised, the Jews would win. But when Moshe got tired and lowered his hands, then Amalek started to win!

But it wasn't that Moshe's hands had a special power. When the Jews saw Moshe with his hands up, they were inspired to turn to Hashem and pray for His help — and Hashem helped.

Moshe sat down on a stone. Chur and Aharon held up his hands and he kept praying.

Victory

Meanwhile, down below, though the Jews were winning, the battle continued. The Amalekite soldiers were not only strong, but they also understood the ancient wisdom of astrology, so they knew at what time of day they would win. That's when they would attack.

The war went on and on until Moshe did something absolutely remarkable — he stopped the sun! This way, the time when the Amalekites would win — would not come! Yehoshua and his men were finally able to defeat the Amalekite army. Yehoshua killed the strongest Amalekite soldiers and let the weak ones go.

The Future

Though Yehoshua had the power to destroy all of the enemy, Hashem told him to just kill the strong ones. The time had not yet come for Amalek to be totally destroyed.

When is the time for Amalek's total destruction? When Mashiach arrives.

Meanwhile Hashem told Moshe to write down the story of how Amalek attacked the Jews for no reason, so the Jews should remember it forever. He was also to tell Yehoshua that the nation of Amalek is the enemy of Hashem, and should be wiped out.

Thank You

An army made of former slaves with no fighting experience defeated the well trained and experienced Amalek forces. That was a miracle!

Moshe was 80 years old and he sat on a stone? Couldn't they find something soft and more comfortable for him?

Moshe didn't want a pillow. He said, "The Jews are suffering, fighting a battle, and I should be comfortable? I'll sit on a stone and suffer with them."

To show appreciation, Moshe built a mizbei'ach to Hashem as a permanent reminder of the miracle. He gave the mizbei'ach a name: "Hashem nisi — Hashem is my miracle."

Hashem Makes a Promise

Because of Amalek's actions Hashem made a promise that there would be a war against Amalek forever. Until Amalek is wiped out, Hashem's Name and His Throne will not be complete.

This means that as long as Amalek's evil is in the world, people will not totally believe in Hashem as Master of the Universe.

Chutzpah!

What was so bad about what Amalek did that they deserved to be wiped out?

The whole world was in awe of Hashem and His people after the miracle of Kriyas Yam Suf. They were afraid of Hashem and His power. Everyone was frightened to fight with the Jews.

Everyone except ... Amalek! Amalek wanted to prove to the world that everything that happened to the Jews, happened by chance. They wanted people to believe that there is no G-d, and that Jews have no special protection. To prove that, they attacked the Jews.

Often, something can seem impossible to do, until one man does it. Then many people try to do it. The Midrash explains:

There is a bathtub of boiling hot water. No one dares go in, because they will get burned! One fool decides to jump in. Ouch, it hurts! He gets burned — but once he went in, he cooled off the water. Now others will jump in.

That's why what Amalek did was so bad. Amalek defied Hashem. After everything Hashem did to show His power! His actions cooled off the world's awe of Hashem and they stopped being afraid of the Jews.

פָּרָשַׁת יִתְרוֹ

❖ Parashas Yisro

Yisro · יִתְרוֹ

Parashah Pointers

▸ Moshe's father-in-law, Yisro, hears about the miracles Hashem did for the Jews — Kriyas Yam Suf, the war with Amalek, the mahn that fell from heaven, and the well that gave them water in the desert.

▸ Yisro takes his daughter Tziporah, Moshe's wife, and their two children, Gershom and Eliezer, to join the Jews in the desert.

▸ Yisro converts to Judaism.

▸ Until now, Moshe was judging all the cases of the Jewish people. Yisro advises him to appoint more judges.

▸ Yisro returns to Midian.

▸ The Aseres HaDibros (Ten Commandments) are given to the Jews at Har Sinai. They are:

   1. "I am Hashem."

   2. Don't believe in idols.

   3. Don't say Hashem's Name for no reason.

   4. Remember the day of Shabbos.

   5. Honor your father and mother.

   6. Do not kill.

   7. Do not marry the wife of another man.

   8. Do not steal.

   9. If you are a witness in court, don't lie.

   10. Don't desire someone else's belongings.

▸ The Torah gives rules to follow when building the Mizbei'ach, the Altar, where korbanos (offerings) were burned.

News

The miracles of Kriyas Yam Suf and the amazing defeat of Amalek by the Jews made news all over the world. But out of all the people in the world who heard the news, the only one who did something because of it was Yisro, Moshe's father-in-law.

Yisro entirely changed his life because of what he heard. He dropped what he was doing, closed up his comfortable home, and headed to the desert to join the Jews. Yisro took along Moshe's wife Tziporah, and their two children, Gershom and Eliezer.

The Message

When Yisro arrived, he stopped at the edge of the Jewish camp. He sent a message to Moshe.

"It is I, your father-in-law, Yisro. I have arrived from Midian with your wife and children. Please come out to welcome me. If not for my sake, do it for the sake of your wife. And if not for her sake, do it for the sake of your children."

Welcome!

As soon as Moshe got the message, he went out to honor his father-in-law and welcome his family. Aharon and his two oldest sons, Nadav and Avihu, went with Moshe. When the Jews saw their leaders going somewhere, they followed along.

Yisro couldn't believe his eyes! Moshe was personally coming out to greet him, along with the leaders of the Jews! Behind them, stretching far into the distance, was the entire Jewish people. What an honor, what a welcome!

Moshe bowed down to the ground to show respect for his father-in-law. Then he got up and gave him a kiss.

Search for Truth

Yisro had been the main priest serving the idols of Midian. He gave up his job because he was searching for the true G-d of the world. Moshe knew that Yisro wasn't coming just for a family visit. He was looking for the true G-d — Hashem — and for His Torah.

FASCINATING FACTS

There is an opinion that Yisro joined the Jews before the giving of the Torah at Har Sinai. Another opinion is that this happened after the Jews had already received the Torah.

QUESTIONS, ANYONE?

Why were Moshe's sons called Gershom and Eliezer?

Moshe named his first son Gershom (which means: "a stranger") because the baby was born when Moshe was living in Midian. He was a stranger in the country, without his family and fellow Jews — the only Jew in the entire country.

His second son, Eliezer (which means "G-d, my Helper"), was named for the miracle that saved Moshe's life. Pharaoh ordered his officer to kill Moshe with a sword. When the sword came crashing down on Moshe's neck — nothing happened! Moshe's neck had turned to marble. (For the whole story see Parashas Shemos, page 10.)

So after welcoming his father-in-law, Moshe brought him straight to the beis midrash, the study hall, where he could help his father-in-law discover more about Hashem. Moshe told him about the miracles that had happened to them at the Yam Suf and the war with Amalek. He spoke to him about the mahn, the food that fell from heaven, and the water that came from a stone. He told him all these things to bring him close to Hashem and Torah.

The Convert

Yisro listened to Moshe's words. He had worshipped every other god, and he now realized that the only true G-d is Hashem. He told Moshe, "Blessed is Hashem Who saved you from Egypt and Pharaoh. Now I know that Hashem is G-d, not the other gods."

He decided to join the Jewish people and become a Jew himself.

The Party

To celebrate becoming a Jew, Yisro brought korbanos to Hashem and made a party. He invited Moshe, Aharon, and the righteous leaders of the Jews to his party. Moshe insisted on working as a waiter at the party. He wanted the mitzvah of serving the guests.

TORAH IN OUR LIVES

Yisro had worked for the Egyptian empire and was even one of Pharaoh's three advisers. So when he heard about all the bad things that happened to Egypt it made him get goosebumps because he was upset. He couldn't help feeling bad, because he used to be in Egypt just like the Egyptians.

This shows us that we should be very careful not to say anything that might hurt someone's feelings.

A Hard Job

Yisro passed a large number of people waiting on line. He asked someone what they were waiting for.

"We are all waiting for our turn to speak to Moshe Rabbeinu," the man answered. "Some of us have questions about how to be a better Jew. Others are arguing about something and they want Moshe to decide who is right."

Yisro could see it would take a very long time till the last Jew in line would have his turn to see Moshe! And how tired Moshe would be by the end of the day!

That night Yisro had a talk with Moshe.

A Good Suggestion

"Your system of judging the Jews isn't working well," Yisro told him. "You can't be the only one to judge the Jews. It's too hard a job for just one man, and why should the Jews have to stand in line for so long? This is my idea. Instead of you doing all the work yourself, share the job with others. Please check with Hashem to see if I'm right."

Moshe + 78,600

This is how Yisro's plan would work.

Yisro told Moshe to appoint many judges, one for every 10 Jews, one for every 50 Jews, one for every 100, and one for every 1,000.

If there is a question of law, the Jew goes to the judge in charge of him and the other nine people. If that judge doesn't know the answer, the question goes to the judge in charge of fifty. If that judge doesn't know the answer, it keeps going up level by level. If no one knows the answer … it goes to Moshe for judgment.

If Moshe doesn't know, what then? Moshe asks Hashem for the answer!

Altogether Moshe was looking for 78,600 people to become judges!

Moshe took Yisro's advice and things got a lot better. Moshe had less of a workload, and the Jews didn't have to wait so long anymore.

What Kind of Judges?

Not anyone can be a good judge. Yisro advised Moshe what kind of people he should appoint as judges.

They should:

▸ be good leaders
▸ be wealthy people who cannot be paid off to make a false judgment
▸ be afraid of Hashem, not of people
▸ be honest
▸ not be interested in money. They should look at money as not important.

QUESTIONS, ANYONE?

The Torah tells us that the party that Yisro made was "before Hashem." In what way was it "before Hashem"?

If tzaddikim are at a meal, Hashem's Presence is also there, so they are eating "before Hashem."

Goodbye

Yisro loved being with the Jews, Moshe, and his family. But he decided to return to Midian. He wanted to teach his children and others about Hashem. He decided to go back and try to convert his family and other Midianites.

Moshe tried to get Yisro to stay. But Yisro had made up his mind.

Moshe sent Yisro off with great honor and many gifts.

Mattan Torah — The Giving of the Torah

The most important day in world history is the day the Torah was given!

If the Jews hadn't accepted the Torah, the world would have disappeared. That makes it the greatest thing that ever happened.

The reason the world exists, the reason it was created, and the reason it still exists, is for people to keep the Torah. Nothing in the world is as great and valuable as our Torah.

The Torah is important for another reason too. Without it we wouldn't know how to use the world the way Hashem wants us to. We wouldn't know how we're supposed to act, how to behave to others, how to make Hashem — and ourselves — happy.

This parashah describes the preparations the Jews made to receive the Torah, and what happened on the day the Torah was given.

The story begins on Rosh Chodesh Sivan, the day the Jews arrived at Har Sinai. This was the mountain where Hashem had spoken to Moshe from the burning bush, telling him it was time to take the Jews out of Egypt.

Day One (Rosh Chodesh Sivan): One Man, One Heart

During the six weeks after the Jews left Egypt they complained to Moshe and Hashem many times. The war against Amalek made the Jews realize how wrong they had been, and they did teshuvah, they repented.

The Jews arrived at Har Sinai on Rosh Chodesh Sivan, the first day of the month of Sivan. On that day, Hashem let them rest from their travels.

QUESTIONS, ANYONE?

Why was the Torah given in a desert?

1. The desert is a place that belongs to no one. Anyone can go there without tickets, without paying to get in. The Torah was given in the desert to show that no matter who you are, the Torah is available for you to learn.

2. The desert is a place with sand dunes stretching for miles in all directions. No trees, no cities, no people. It seems endless. The reward for learning and keeping Torah is also endless. Our imagination is not big enough to understand how much reward there is for learning even a small amount of Torah.

At Sinai there were no more complaints. All the Jews were at peace with one another. They loved one another like brothers and sisters. There was only one thing they all wanted more than anything else — the Torah.

All three million Jews were like one person with one heart. They were united with each other, and united in their desire to receive the Torah.

Day Two (Sivan 2): The Question

Moshe went up Har Sinai where Hashem spoke to him. Hashem sent Moshe with a message to the people: "Do you really want the Torah?" Hashem instructed Moshe to first ask the women, in a nice and pleasant way. With the men he should talk more firmly. He should let them know the Torah comes with great responsibilities. Did they still want it?

Just Like an Eagle

This was Hashem's message:
"You saw with your own eyes how I punished the Egyptians and how I took you out of Egypt. Remember how on the day you left Egypt you were spread out all over Goshen, and suddenly, miraculously, you found yourselves all together at Ramses, ready to leave Egypt.

"When the Egyptians were chasing you I sent a pillar-shaped cloud to capture all the arrows that they shot at you. I protected you like an eagle protects her children by carrying them on her wings, so that any arrows shot from below will hit her and not her young."

Promise for the Future

Hashem told them:
"If you accept My Torah you will be an 'am segulah,' a beloved treasure to Me. I will watch over you, the way a king's treasure house is always watched and protected. You will be My most loved nation on earth, My special nation.

"You will be a nation of Kohanim, who inspire others to be good and serve Hashem. You will become leaders who will lead the world to believe in Me and to be good.

"You will be a holy nation that cares more about spiritual things like mitzvos, chessed, and Torah study, instead of being focused on money and physical pleasure."

QUESTIONS, ANYONE?

Why did Hashem tell Moshe to speak to the women first?

Because the mothers, who raise their young children, will be the first to teach them Torah.

FASCINATING FACTS

Hashem promised that we would be a nation of Kohanim. If they hadn't sinned with the Eigel HaZahav (see p. 160), all Jews would have been like Kohanim. They too would have been able to eat all types of the korbanos that Kohanim may eat. (There are some korbanos that everyone may eat, and others that only Kohanim may eat. Some have to be burned completely and no one may eat them.) After the sin of the Eigel HaZahav, only Kohanim could eat certain korbanos.

The Answer

Moshe came down from Har Sinai, where Hashem had been talking to him. He gathered together the Jewish people. Moshe seated the great wise men of Israel and told the people Hashem's message.

As soon as the Jews heard Moshe telling the wise men Hashem's message, they all spoke up and said, "Everything Hashem said we agree to! We'll do it!"

A Smart Choice!

What a smart nation! If Hashem is giving something away you take it, no questions asked. The Jews trusted their Creator. They knew He wanted what is best for them.

Think about it: A father comes home with a beautifully wrapped present in his hand. He offers it to his child. Would the child think to ask, "I'm not sure I want it. Let me see what it is"? Of course not.

But the other nations of the world weren't as smart as the Jews.

Not for Us

Hashem wanted to be fair to all the nations, so before offering it to the Jews, He offered the Torah to them as well.

He went to the nation whose founder was Eisav and asked them, "Do you want the Torah?"

What did they answer? Unlike the Jews, they asked, "What does it say?"

Hashem answered, "You are not allowed to kill."

"No thanks," they said, "it's not for us. Killing is part of our culture."

Hashem tried the nations who were descendants of Yishmael. They also asked, "What does this Torah say?"

Hashem said, "You are not allowed to steal."

"Not for us. Stealing is part of our culture."

The same thing happened with all the 70 nations that Hashem offered the Torah to. Not one of them understood that if Hashem is giving you something, you don't have to ask questions. You take it, because it's the best thing in the world for you.

Day Three (Sivan 3): See the King

Moshe went up the next morning to bring back the Jews' answer to Hashem. "Yes, they want the Torah."

Hashem told Moshe that He would speak to him from a thick cloud to give the Torah. The Jews would hear Hashem's voice speaking to Moshe. When they heard that, they would know that Hashem spoke to Moshe. And all future generations would know forever that Moshe was Hashem's prophet.

Moshe went down from Har Sinai and told the Jews what to expect. They were not happy about it at all. But this time their complaint was a good one.

They asked, "Why should we hear the Torah from Moshe, G-d's messenger? We love Hashem, we want to be close to Him. We want to hear the Torah directly from Hashem. We want to see our King!"

The Jews just wanted more holiness!

Off Limits!

Har Sinai would be off limits to the Jews. Because of Hashem's strong Presence on the mountain, no one — neither human nor animal — was allowed to touch the mountain. Someone who touched the mountain would die.

To keep the Jews off Har Sinai, Hashem told Moshe they were not allowed to touch the mountain until they would hear a loud shofar blast. That would be a signal that Hashem's Presence had left the mountain and it was now once again permitted to go up Har Sinai.

Day Four (Sivan 4): Get Ready

Hashem was very pleased when Moshe told Him what the Jews said. But in order for Hashem to speak to them directly, they would have to prepare. They would have to make themselves very holy.

They were told to make themselves and their clothes spiritually pure by going to the mikvah. To stay pure for the next three days, they would have to keep from touching anything that is tamei (impure).

On the sixth day of Sivan — they would receive the Torah!

TORAH IN OUR LIVES

The tall mountains thought the Torah should be given on them, because they were show-offs and proud to be so tall. But Hashem chose Har Sinai, because it was small and humble. This shows that the Torah only stays with a person who is humble and doesn't show off.

Day Five (Sivan 5):

or more details on what happened on the fifth day, see Parashas Mishpatim, page 113.

The Miracles at Sinai

hat would a young boy — let's call him Eliezer — have heard and experienced on that unforgettable day of Mattan Torah?

Overslept

liezer is sleeping in his tent in the desert. He wakes up suddenly to the loud sounds of booming thunder. His eyes pop open. "Oh no, I've overslept! Hashem is giving the Torah today! If I don't hurry I'll miss it!"

As he jumps into his clothes he can hear Moshe's voice waking up the Jewish people, telling them to hurry up and get to Har Sinai because Hashem is waiting to give us the Torah. Eliezer feels better. He did not oversleep. What happened was that Hashem came earlier than everyone expected.

Fire and Smoke

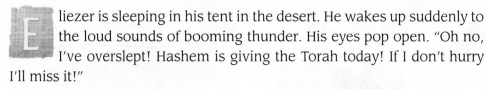

ll dressed, Eliezer steps out of the tent and looks at the mountain. It's a frightening sight. The mountain is covered with so much smoke and fire. Above it are flashes of lightning. A thick cloud hangs over it. The very earth of the mountain is moving, shaking and trembling.

The mountain itself is surrounded with greenery. Amazing — this is out here in the desert! Yesterday it was just a barren, rocky mountain. Now, it is completely surrounded by greenery and it is beautiful.

No Illness

liezer starts running toward Har Sinai, and sees his friend Asher running right past him, giving him a quick wave. Asher was the quickest runner of all his friends until his accident. When Asher was a slave in Egypt, a large stone fell on him and broke his leg. Since the accident, Asher has always limped, and walking was hard for him. Now he's running!

Looking around, Eliezer sees a neighbor who had lost an arm in Egypt. He's got both arms now. There is his cousin Shimon, who'd been blinded by a cruel, Jew-hating Egyptian. He's not blind anymore.

Before giving the Torah, Hashem healed all the sick Jews, so that everyone could see and hear what He had to say, and so that everyone would be at Mattan Torah with healthy bodies.

When all the Jews are gathered around the mountain, Eliezer hears the sound of a shofar blast. It's not a regular shofar blast. A shofar blast usually starts out very loud and then gets quieter and softer as the person blowing the shofar gets out of breath. This one, though, gets louder and louder. There is no person blowing this shofar. It is a Heavenly shofar blast.

TORAH IN OUR LIVES

How do you know George Washington was a real person, and that the American Revolution really happened? Everyone knows it's true because the Americans alive at the time of the Revolution were there when it happened. Many people actually met President Washington. They wrote it down and told their children about it. If it was all made up, the people living at the time would have said the whole thing is a fake story.

We are the only religion in the world that says that Hashem came and spoke, not just to Moshe or to a few people, but to the whole nation of three million people. How can it not be true? All the people who were alive at Mattan Torah then told their children exactly what happened, who told their children — up to this very day!

QUESTIONS, ANYONE?

Which number keeps coming up again and again at Mattan Torah?

Three. The Torah was given in the third month, Sivan.

It was given through Moshe, the third child of Yocheved.

It was given to all three parts of the Jewish people: Kohen, Levi, Yisrael.

The written Torah itself has three parts: Torah, Nevi'im, Kesuvim (Torah, Prophets, Writings).

One of the many reasons for this is because the Torah came in the merit of our three forefathers: Avraham, Yitzchak, and Yaakov.

Silence

oshe comes down the mountain. He tells all the Jews that Hashem sent him down to warn them once again not to go near Har Sinai.

Eliezer suddenly hears … nothing. A deep silence falls upon the world. The birds are quiet, there is no roar of the ocean's waves. All the animals stand still. No purring, no roaring, no growling. Not one word is spoken. The world is absolutely silent.

Hashem is about to speak.

Hashem Speaks

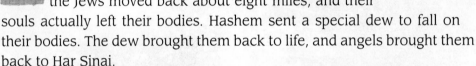

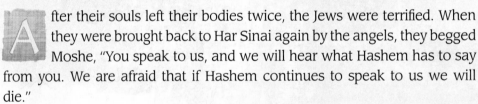

When Hashem said His first command, "I am Hashem, your G-d," it was so powerful that the Jews moved back about eight miles, and their souls actually left their bodies. Hashem sent a special dew to fall on their bodies. The dew brought them back to life, and angels brought them back to Har Sinai.

The powerful voice of Hashem was heard again. It was the second command, "You must not have any other god." The same thing happened to the Jews that happened to them the first time.

Worried to Death

After their souls left their bodies twice, the Jews were terrified. When they were brought back to Har Sinai again by the angels, they begged Moshe, "You speak to us, and we will hear what Hashem has to say from you. We are afraid that if Hashem continues to speak to us we will die."

"Hashem doesn't want you to die," Moshe said. "He spoke to you to make you famous, as the only nation that Hashem ever talked to. Also, after seeing how powerful and awesome Hashem is, you will be afraid of Him and won't sin."

Moshe Speaks to the Jews

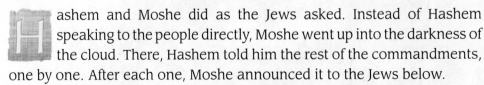

Hashem and Moshe did as the Jews asked. Instead of Hashem speaking to the people directly, Moshe went up into the darkness of the cloud. There, Hashem told him the rest of the commandments, one by one. After each one, Moshe announced it to the Jews below.

How could three million Jews hear Moshe speaking? Even if he spoke in a very loud voice, the Jews in the back would not have been able to hear him! What happened was that Hashem made Moshe's voice loud enough for all three million Jews to hear every word he said.

It Happened at Sinai

The Torah was given on a Shabbos, in the month of Sivan, 2448 years after the world was created.

Here is a list of some other fascinating things that happened on that great day of Mattan Torah.

▸ Hashem picked up Har Sinai and held it in the air over the heads of the entire Jewish nation. He told them: "Either accept the Torah, or you will be buried under the mountain when it drops."

▸ Hashem didn't come down alone. Along with Him came an honor guard of 22,000 angels.

▸ The Jews not only heard the voice of Hashem, but somehow they were able to see the words He spoke as well.

▸ Many years before, Hashem tested Avraham by asking him to sacrifice his son Yitzchak. At the last moment Hashem sent an angel to stop Avraham from sacrificing his son. Avraham offered a ram instead.

The shofar blast the Jews heard at Har Sinai came from the shofar made from the left horn of Avraham Avinu's ram. When Mashiach comes to end our present exile, we will hear a blast from a shofar made from the same ram's right horn. May we hear that shofar blast very soon!

▸ Did it ever happen to you that after a class the students argue about what the teacher said?

After the Aseres HaDibros were given, the Jews discussed them and every Jew heard exactly what the other heard. There was no disagreement between the three million people who were at Sinai as to what Hashem had said.

▸ Before saying each of the commandments separately, Hashem said all of them at the same time, something no human can do.

FASCINATING FACTS

The numerical value of the Hebrew word "Torah" (תּוֹרָה) is 611. If we add the two commandments that Hashem spoke to the Jews directly, not through Moshe, we get 613. 613 is the total number of mitzvos in the Torah.

There is a hint of that in the famous verse that says (Devarim 33:4): "Torah tzivah lanu Moshe — Moshe commanded us the Torah." From Moshe we got the Torah — that is, 611 mitzvos. The other two we heard directly from Hashem.

QUESTIONS, ANYONE?

When the Torah tells us to remember Shabbos, what does it mean?

There are a few ways we do this mitzvah.

▸ The most important one is to make Kiddush, announcing that it's Shabbos today.

▸ If when you are shopping you come across something really special or new or tasty, instead of buying it to eat for dinner that night, save it for Shabbos. That's another way to "remember" Shabbos.

When we make Kiddush and keep Shabbos, we are reminding ourselves and the world that Hashem created the world in six days and rested on the seventh.

FASCINATING FACTS

When Hashem said the fourth commandment, He told the Jews to remember and also to guard the Shabbos. He said the words zachor (remember) and shamor (guard) together in the same moment, something no human can do.

The number of letters in the Aseres HaDibros is 620. That's no coincidence. The Torah has 613 mitzvos, and the Rabbis established seven mitzvos = 620.

The seven Rabbinical mitzvos* are:

1. Saying Hallel on certain holidays
2. Saying berachos
3. Washing hands before eating bread
4. Eruv on Shabbos
5. Lighting Shabbos candles
6. Reading Megillas Esther on Purim
7. Lighting the Chanukah menorah

This is a commonly accepted opinion of what these 7 mitzvos are. There are other opinions as well.

Aseres HaDibros / The Ten Commandments

Here are the Aseres HaDibros that the Jews were given at Sinai, together with a short explanation:

1. **I am Hashem, your G-d, Who took you out of Egypt.** (Even though we cannot see Hashem, we must believe He exists.)

2. **Don't believe in any other gods. Don't make statues of anything in heaven or on earth. Don't bow to or pray to idols. If you do, you will be punished for four generations** (if the children sin like their parents). **But the reward for loving Me and keeping My mitzvos and doing good deeds will last for two thousand generations.**

3. **Don't disgrace Hashem's Name by using it when you swear about something foolish or for no reason.** (Like swearing in His Name that a piece of wood is a piece of wood. Or swearing that a rock is really a chunk of plastic.)

4. **Remember and keep the Shabbos to be a holy day. Work during the six days of the week. The seventh day, Shabbos, should be devoted to Hashem**.

   No one may work on Shabbos — not you, your children, animals, or slaves. Because Hashem created the world in six days and rested on the seventh. That's why Hashem blessed the Shabbos and made it holy.

5. **Honor your father and mother and you will live long.**

6. **Don't kill.**

7. **Do not marry the wife of another man.**

8. **Don't steal.** (You are not allowed to kidnap someone and force him to work for you and then sell him as a slave.)

9. **If you are a witness in the court, don't say anything that isn't true.**

10. **Don't wish you could have someone else's things.**

Last Words

After giving the Aseres HaDibros, Hashem told Moshe that He will tell the Jews to make Keruvim. These were two gold statues to be put on the Aron that contained the Aseres HaDibros. These were the only statues that the Jews were allowed to make. They had to be of gold, not silver or any other material. No copies may be made for shuls or anywhere else.

Iron Kills

The parashah ends with rules for making the Mizbei'ach, on which the Jews would bring korbanos in the Mishkan. It was made of a hollow box filled with earth. (For more details, see Parashas Terumah, page 136.)

The Mizbei'ach in the Beis HaMikdash was to be made of stones. The stones could not be cut and shaped with iron tools, because weapons such as daggers and swords are made out of iron. Weapons shorten life, they kill. The Mizbei'ach brought long and good lives to the Jews, by bringing blessing and forgiveness.

To get to the top of the Mizbei'ach, the Kohanim should walk on a ramp, not stairs.

The Torah tells us more about Mattan Torah at the end of Parashas Mishpatim. (See Parashas Mishpatim, page 113.)

Why did Hashem want a ramp instead of stairs?

To teach us about modesty and respecting others. The Kohanim wore a long ankle-length robe. If they would use steps, their underclothing would be exposed to the stones below them as they walked up. Out of respect for the Mizbei'ach, and because of modesty, Hashem told us to make a ramp.

Of course, stones don't have feelings. But Hashem wants us to see that if He was so careful about something that has no feelings, we should certainly be careful when we deal with people, who do have feelings. We must never hurt someone's feelings.

פָּרָשַׁת מִשְׁפָּטִים

◆

Parashas Mishpatim

Mishpatim · מִשְׁפָּטִים

Parashah Pointers

▸ After Mattan Torah, Moshe taught the Jews many laws of the Torah. Here are some of the laws Moshe taught them.

- Laws of the Jewish bondsman (someone who beis din sold to work as if he were a slave)

- Payments for hurting or damaging others

- To return lost items

- Treat a convert, orphan, or widow with kindness

- Lend money without interest

- Don't cook milk and meat together

▸ The parashah then tells us what happened on the two days before the Torah was given at Sinai, and on the day after.

- Two days before the Torah was given, Moshe told the Jews to prepare themselves by becoming tahor, pure. He also taught them some mitzvos.

- One day before the Torah was given, Moshe built a mizbei'ach. The Jews said, "Naaseh v'nishma! We will do and we will hear." Hashem rewarded each Jew with two heavenly crowns.

- The day after the Aseres HaDibros were given, Moshe went up to Shamayim for 40 days and nights, so Hashem could teach him the Torah.

The Torah's Laws

The story of what happened at Mattan Torah that we read about last week isn't over yet. At the end of this parashah, the Torah continues telling the fascinating story of what happened to the Jews at Har Sinai. You can skip to page 113 to read more about the awesome events that happened at Har Sinai.

The beginning of the parashah discusses the laws Moshe taught after Mattan Torah.

Let's begin with the laws of how a beis din (a Jewish court) should pass judgment. Every country has courts, judges, and law books. But there is a huge difference between our laws and theirs, our courts and theirs.

Beis Din

When a beis din passes judgment according to the Torah, it is doing a mitzvah, Hashem's will. Therefore, judges have to work hard learning Torah in order to know how to judge cases according to the halachah. Learning is the greatest mitzvah.

The laws of the beis din appear right after the giving of the Torah at Sinai to teach us that these laws are part of the Torah, just like all the other mitzvos given at Sinai. Keeping Shabbos or judging how much money a person who hurts someone else should pay are both mitzvos. They are both holy.

As a matter of fact, when judges in beis din rule fairly according to the Torah, Hashem Himself comes down to be with them. Not only that, but Hashem says that an honest judge is like His partner in creating the world!

How Important Is It to Judge Fairly?

The laws of being a fair judge come right after the laws about the Mizbei'ach. The Sanhedrin, which was the highest court in Eretz Yisrael, was located right next to the Beis HaMikdash, near the Mizbei'ach. This teaches us that judging fairly is just as important to Hashem as serving Him in the Beis HaMikdash.

A Jewish Servant

If a Jew was caught stealing and he didn't have money to pay back, he was sold as a "bondsman," similar to a slave, who must work as a servant for six years, or until Yovel,* whichever comes first.

Now, who would buy a servant who is a thief? Who would bring him into their home? Only a Jew who cares enough about another Jew to help him stop being a thief.

Every 50th year is called Yovel. In that year, farmers do not work the land and many laws are associated with the Yovel year. Yovel was marked only when all the shevatim lived on their territories in Eretz Yisrael.

FASCINATING FACTS

Our laws are made by Hashem, not by people. Because Hashem made them, they are always 100% fair.

FASCINATING FACTS

Many of the great heroes of Jewish history were judges, including Moshe Rabbeinu, Shmuel HaNavi, King David, and King Shlomo. Even Mashiach will be a judge.

Today, many of our Jewish leaders also serve as judges. They work hard to make peace between Jews who are arguing over money or other issues, and deciding who is right.

When two Jews have a disagreement over money or anything else, they are not allowed to go to a non-Jewish court to judge their case. It is a chillul Hashem, an act that is insulting to Hashem, to do such a thing! It's like saying that the court is smarter than the Torah.

Why is the servant's ear pierced?

Because it was his ear that heard the commandment at Har Sinai not to steal. But he went and stole anyway, so we put a hole in his ear.

Once the thief becomes a servant, he works only for his master. But his master has to treat him well. He may not be given work that would embarrass him. If the master has only one pillow — the servant gets it! Whatever the master eats, the servant eats, too. If the thief is married, the master must support his entire family.

By the time the six years are over, hopefully the thief has learned his lesson. He will leave his criminal ways and start a new and better life.

This law is in force only when Jews live in Eretz Yisrael and Yovel is celebrated.

The Happy Servant

As we just explained, if a Jew stole from someone and doesn't have the money to pay back what he stole, the beis din "sells" him to be a servant. He has to work for six years or until the Yovel year, whichever comes first.

What if the servant is so happy where he is, that after six years he does not want to leave? He is allowed to stay on, but first he and his master must come to beis din. They tell the court that the servant does not want to go free. The servant says twice: "I love my master, my wife, and my children." Beis din will instruct his master to stand the servant next to a door and make a hole in his right ear. The servant stays with the master until Yovel, and then he goes free.

THE LAWS OF DAMAGES AND SHOMRIM

The Torah now discusses the laws of what happens if someone hurts another person or damages property, and if someone was taking care of someone else's property.

Injury

Here is an example of how beis din deals with injuries:

Yosef Gross hit Heshy Klein. Heshy, a 60-year-old man, fell and broke his arm. How would the beis din calculate how much money Mr. Gross has to pay him?

The beis din will charge Mr. Gross for five things:

▸ **Nezek (damages):** *The price difference between what Heshy Klein would be worth if he was sold as a slave when he was well, and how much he is worth now with the broken arm.*

▸ **Tzaar (pain):** *How much would this man pay someone to give him a less painful way to break his arm. Let's say someone needs to have his arm broken, for a good reason. How much would he pay for a pill that makes him not feel the pain of the arm being broken?*

- **Ripui (medical expenses):** *All medical expenses that need to be paid to heal the broken arm.*

- **Sheves (unemployment):** *He gets minimum wage for the days he was out of work.*

- **Boshes (embarrassment):** *It's embarrassing to be hit and be lying in the street, screaming in pain from a broken arm! Beis din makes Yosef pay for embarrassing Heshy.*

Holes in the Street

Someone who digs a hole in the street or removes the cover on a pit in the street is responsible for damage if someone falls in and gets hurt. We are also not allowed to leave dangerous things in the street, like broken glass, or things that people can trip over. If someone does that, he is responsible for any damage he caused to the person, but not for the damages to his belongings and the clothing that he is wearing.

2, 4, 5

If a thief is caught, beis din makes him pay back the owners two times what he stole. For example, if he stole a bike worth $350, the thief has to return the bike — and pay the owner an extra $350.

There are some exceptions. If he stole a sheep, and killed it or sold it, he pays the sheep's owner four times the value of the sheep. (If he still has the sheep, he pays back double.) If he stole an ox, and killed or sold it, he has to pay five times as much as it was worth.

Four, Not Five

Why does the thief pay more for the ox than for the sheep? Imagine stealing a sheep. The thief can't just stuff it into a bag like he would if he was stealing jewelry. He has to pick the sheep up, put it on his shoulders, and leave the barn. When he gets outside, he can't just put the sheep down. It will run away. So the thief has to look like a fool, carrying a sheep through the street on his shoulders.

But if he steals an ox, the ox just walks on its own. The thief doesn't have to carry it on his shoulders. Because the one who stole the sheep felt some embarrassment, Hashem makes him pay only four times as much. The thief who stole an ox was not embarrassed, so he pays five times the ox's worth.

Half and Whole

t is unusual for an ox to gore another animal (that is, to hit him with his sharp horns), or to purposefully run into a person or animal. If he does, the first three times the ox's owner has to pay for only half the damages his animal caused. But if the ox gored animals more than three times, and the ox's owner has been warned that his ox is dangerous, he knows that he has to guard it better. When that ox gores another animal, its owner pays for the full cost of the damage his ox did to the other animal.

Fire!

f a person started a fire and wasn't careful with it, he must pay for any damage done by the fire.

Let's say Shimon makes a bonfire to roast hot dogs or marshmallows in his backyard. Then he goes back into the house to get something.

A disaster happens. The fire spreads and is burning down his neighbor's house.

Fortunately, no one was hurt. But Shimon has to pay his neighbor for all the damage his fire caused.

Careful!

he Torah teaches us that fires are dangerous. They can go out of control all by themselves. So when making a BBQ, campfire or fire to burn chametz, take fire safety rules seriously! Always have plenty of water around in case the fire starts to get out of control. Before you leave the area, make sure the fire and all the coals are extinguished. And never, ever leave a fire without someone there to watch it.

Laws of "Shomrim"

Here are three legal questions that can come up:

Question 1: Shmuli is traveling to Eretz Yisrael. Avraham gives Shmuli a piece of luggage to give to Avraham's son in Yerushalayim. The airline loses the luggage. Does Shmuli have to pay Avraham for the luggage?

Question 2: What if someone paid Yosef to watch his bike. Yosef put it in his garage, and the bike is stolen. Does Yosef have to pay for the bike?

Question 3: Chaya borrows a mixer to bake cookies, and while she is using it, the bowl cracks. Does Chaya have to pay for the bowl?

The answers to these questions are found in the laws of **shomrim** — people who are asked to care for something that belongs to someone else. Read the laws that follow, and then try to answer the questions.

A person who is asked to safeguard something is called a **shomer**. This includes someone who borrows an item, or rents it, because he is responsible to safeguard the items he is using.

There are four kinds of shomrim:

1. Shomer Chinam

A **shomer chinam** is given something to watch over till the owner returns for it. The shomer is doing it for free, as a favor to the owner.

Some of the laws of the shomer chinam are:

▸ If what he was watching was stolen or lost (say, the airline lost his luggage) or broken, and it wasn't his fault, he doesn't have to pay.

▸ When there are no witnesses that it was lost or stolen, the shomer chinam swears in beis din that it wasn't his fault. He also swears that he never used what he was watching for himself and that he doesn't have it. If he does this, he doesn't have to pay the owner.

2. Shomer Sachar

A **shomer sachar** is paid to watch over an item until the owner comes for it.

Some of the laws of the shomer sachar are:

▸ If the item was lost or stolen, he must pay for it. But if it was lost or stolen because of something that happened beyond his control — for example, if the item was lost in an earthquake or a bandit held him up with a gun — and he has witnesses to prove it — he doesn't have to pay.

▸ If there are no witnesses, he has to swear in beis din that something happened beyond his control. He also swears that he never used what he was watching for himself, and that he doesn't have the item.

3. Sachir

A **sachir** is someone who rents something.
The laws of the sachir are the same as the shomer sachar. (See above.)

4. Shoel

A **shoel** is someone who borrows something.

Some of the laws of the shoel are:

▸ If the item was lost, stolen, or broken by accident, the borrower has to pay, even if what happened was beyond his control. The exception is if the borrowed item broke when he was using it normally. For example, David borrows a hammer from Danny, and when he uses it to pound a nail into the wall — it breaks. Then he doesn't have to pay Danny for the hammer.

▸ If the borrowed item was lost or stolen while its owner was working together with the borrower, the borrower pays nothing. For example, David borrows a hammer from Danny. David is working for Danny, painting his house (there is no difference if David is doing it for pay or for free) and the hammer is stolen. David doesn't have to pay for it.

Back to the Questions

Remember those three questions we asked? Now go back, and try to figure out what kind of shomer each of them is — and if they have to pay or not.

Question 1: Shmuli is a shomer chinam. He wasn't paid to watch the luggage, so he doesn't pay for it when it got lost.

Question 2: Yosef is a shomer sachar. He is obligated to pay if the bike gets stolen.

Question 3: Chaya is a shoel, a borrower. She used the mixer in the regular way, so she doesn't have to pay for the damage.

Be Careful

Besides being careful with people's property, we also have to be very careful how we treat anyone. We have to be nice to others, and not say something that might hurt their feelings. Certainly, we should never take advantage of anyone.

The Torah warns us to be especially careful about how we treat widows, orphans, and converts. Why? Because they feel there is no one to protect them. The widow has no husband to stand up for her. An orphan has no father or mother to take care of him, and a convert has no Jewish relatives to help him.

Don't Get Him Angry

Who is known as the Father of the orphans and the Defender of the widows? Hashem Himself. So if someone makes them feel bad and they cry out to Hashem in pain, He gets angry. Hashem punishes the one who caused them to suffer.

Kindness

The poor are called "Hashem's people." That is why there are special laws to make things easier for the poor. Even if someone is temporarily in need, we should help him. Imagine your friend forgot his lunch money. No sandwich, soda, or snack the whole day! You lend him money so he can buy food. Not only are you being nice — you are doing a mitzvah as well!

Hashem commands us that if someone needs a loan, you should be kind and give it to him. You may not charge him interest (extra money) for using the money you lent him. Don't make him return a penny more than what you gave him!

Not only that. If he doesn't pay you when he is supposed to, and you know that he doesn't have the money to pay you — don't ask him for the money! Don't embarrass him by stopping him in the street or going to his house and demanding the money. You know he doesn't have it, so don't ask for it.

FASCINATING FACTS

It is so important to treat a convert properly that the Torah warns us to treat a convert nicely … 36 separate times!

It is not permitted to talk badly about non-Jews in front of a convert because it might make him feel bad.

Wheels and Wealth

Imagine you put a sticker on a bicycle wheel. As you ride, the sticker will sometimes be up and sometimes down as the wheel turns.

Our Sages tell us that being a rich man is like that. A person can be on top of the world — wealthy, living in a mansion, driving an expensive car, honored by everyone. Suddenly something happens and he loses all of his money. The rich man is now at the bottom. No car, no house, no honor. The only way he can manage to feed himself and his family, and try to rebuild his fortune, is if someone lends him money.

What's the reward for giving loans and charity to the poor?

The givers are saved from the punishment of Gehinnom.

FASCINATING FACTS

Giving charity or lending money to the poor without interest is such a great mitzvah that a person gets rewarded for doing this, as if he had done all the 613 mitzvos. That's amazing!

If someone never lies he is given a special power. If he blesses others … the blessing comes true.

TORAH IN OUR LIVES

There is no question that the temptation to cheat is sometimes strong. Copying an answer on a test from someone else is a type of lying. You are pretending you know something, but you really don't. It's a lie!

The next time you want to cheat on an exam, ask yourself: Do you want a better mark, or would you rather be close to Hashem? It's all up to you. It is always your choice.

If you decide not to cheat, and get a lower mark, you might want to tell your parents or your rebbi / morah that you chose not to cheat. They will be proud of you. More important: The Creator of the world will be proud of you.

That's something people should remember. Even if you are rich and can give someone a loan today, tomorrow you may become poor and need a loan yourself. The sticker on the wheel goes up and down!

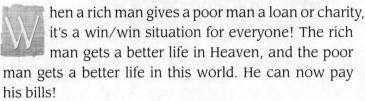
Win / Win

When a rich man gives a poor man a loan or charity, it's a win/win situation for everyone! The rich man gets a better life in Heaven, and the poor man gets a better life in this world. He can now pay his bills!

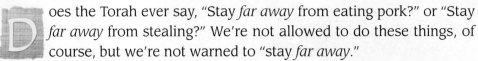
Tell the Truth!

Does the Torah ever say, "Stay *far away* from eating pork?" or "Stay *far away* from stealing?" We're not allowed to do these things, of course, but we're not warned to "stay *far away*."

But when it tells us not to lie, the Torah says "midvar sheker tirchak — stay 'far away' from saying a lie." Lying is so bad, that it gets such a strict warning! The Torah wants us to say only the truth.

Truth is so important that it is one of the three things that allows the world to continue to exist. The other two are justice and peace. So when we tell the truth, we keep the world going. Lies bring destruction.

Kushta

There is a huge reward for people who tell the truth — they will live long. The Gemara tells us about the unusual city of Kushta. Everyone who lived there was very, very careful to tell only the truth. As a result, no one in the city died young.

Hashem does not want to be around a liar. Telling the truth brings people closer to Hashem. Telling a lie pushes them away from Hashem.

The Baal Shem Tov and the Alter of Kelm taught that if you want to become a great Jew … be very careful not to lie.

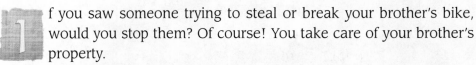
Perikah — Take It Down

If you saw someone trying to steal or break your brother's bike, would you stop them? Of course! You take care of your brother's property.

All Jews are brothers, which is why we are commanded to fulfill the mitzvah called perikah. That is the mitzvah to help unload an animal that will collapse under the heavy load it is carrying. If the animal isn't unloaded, it will collapse. We have to take care of other people's property as if it is our own, making sure it doesn't get damaged.

Cats and Dogs

Hashem doesn't want us to mistreat animals. Before animal owners sit down and eat, they have to make sure their animals have food. The Torah does not want animals to suffer, which is another reason it commanded us to help unload an animal that will collapse under its load.

Conquest

Hashem told the Jews all the wonderful things that would happen to them when they conquer Eretz Yisrael. He will send a powerful angel to protect them. The seven Canaanite nations living in Eretz Yisrael will be conquered, and the Jews will occupy the country.

To help them conquer the Canaanites, Hashem promised to send a very special battalion of poisonous insects — the dreaded tzirah. These insects would shoot poison into the eyes of the Canaanites, who would die from the poison.

No Peace!

Hashem commanded the Jews that when they conquer Eretz Yisrael they have a mission: To destroy all the Canaanite idols. The Jews should NOT make any peace deals with the Canaanites that would allow them to continue living in our holy land. If the Jews allowed the Canaanites to remain, they would cause the Jews to serve worthless idols.

Real Peace

The Jews were promised that if they fulfilled their mission to listen to Hashem and to send away the Canaanite nations, Hashem will bless them. They will live in Eretz Yisrael in peace and happiness. There will be enough food, no illness, and Jews will live long lives. Enemies will be afraid to attack and the Jews will defeat their enemies.

Not So Fast

It would not be good if the Jews would conquer the entire country all at once. If there were areas where people did not live, wild animals would move in. All sorts of wild animals would make their homes all over this empty property.

So Hashem told the Jews that they would not conquer the land right away. It would take seven years to conquer and another seven to divide and settle it. That way the land will be conquered slowly, and the Jews will have enough time for people to move in and get settled.

How long did the conquest actually take? Seven years.

What is Hashem's "seal"?

The Gemara tells us that "emes" (truth) is Hashem's "seal." Of course, Hashem doesn't have a seal that He uses to stamp things. This is the Gemara's way of letting us know the importance of truth.

Can a Jew go hunting for sport?

According to many opinions it is not allowed. For food? Yes. For fun? No.

Did you ever see kids running after stray cats and dogs, screaming at them and making them scared? Causing animals to suffer is called "tzaar baalei chaim." It's wrong. Don't do it!

This parashah (23:20) says that the Jews will be brought "to a place that I made ready." The Midrash explains that this is talking about the Heavenly Beis HaMikdash, which stands above the Beis HaMikdash in Yerushalayim.

A Treasure Chest of Mitzvos

Opening Parashas Mishpatim is like discovering a treasure chest. But this chest isn't filled with gold coins. It's filled with something better — mitzvos! According to the Sefer HaChinuch, which explains all the mitzvos, there are 53 mitzvos in Parashas Mishpatim. We have gone over many of them already. Below are some more!

▸ We are not allowed to curse or hit a parent.

▸ We are used to calling food like crabs, pigs, and snails "treife" (that is, not kosher). But in the Torah, the word "treifah" means a kosher animal or bird that is missing a part of its body or has a sickness that will cause it to die within a year. For example, if a kosher animal has a hole in its heart or is missing a leg. The insides of every kosher animal are checked in the factory by mashgichim, kashrus supervisors, who make sure the animal is not a treifah.

▸ If we find a lost item that has a siman (an identifying sign) on it, like a name or an unusual mark, we must try to find the owner and return it.

▸ It's not permitted to cook meat and milk together. The Torah repeats this command in two other places as well, to teach us that not only is cooking milk and meat forbidden, but we are not allowed to eat it or have benefit from it — like selling it to a non-Jew or feeding it to our non-Jewish servants or to our animals.

▸ On Pesach, Shavuos, and Succos the Jews were supposed to come to the Beis HaMikdash. Imagine how awesome it looked on Succos, with hundreds of thousands of Jews coming to the Beis HaMikdash holding their lulavim and esrogim. Or on Pesach, when Yerushalayim was full of people leading their lambs for the Korban Pesach. On Shavuos they came with their baskets of Bikkurim, the first fruits to ripen in their fields.

When the Jews came they were required to bring animal offerings to the Beis HaMikdash.

More About Mattan Torah

At the end of the parashah, the Torah tells us more of the story of what happened in the days before the Torah was given.*

Another example of this is in Sefer Bereishis. The Torah tells us that Avraham's father, Terach, died, and then it tells us that Avraham went to Eretz Yisrael. In fact, Terach was still alive when Avraham went to Eretz Yisrael.

Two Days Before

Two days before the Torah was given, Hashem told Moshe to go up Har Sinai with his brother Aharon and Aharon's oldest sons, Nadav and Avihu, and the 70 Jewish wise men. However, only Moshe was allowed to go into the thick cloud on top of the mountain, where Hashem's Presence was the strongest.

Hashem told Moshe to go down and tell the Jews to prepare to receive the Torah. They should keep themselves and their clothes spiritually pure by going to the mikvah, and they should stay pure for the next three days by not touching anything that is tamei, impure.

Writing the Torah

Moshe came down with Hashem's message and also taught the Jews some mitzvos. These were the seven commandments that non-Jews must keep, and the mitzvos the Jews had already been given in Marah. (See Parashas Beshalach, page 74.)

After hearing what Moshe told them, all the Jews answered, "Whatever Hashem says, we will do!"

Then Moshe went to his tent where he wrote the first part of the Torah. He wrote everything from Bereishis until that day, the fourth day of Sivan.

An Awesome Day

The next day was awesome. It was the day when the Jews would make an unbreakable agreement with Hashem. We would promise that we would keep the Torah, and Hashem would promise to keep us as His nation. Forever!

This is how the Jews made their agreement with Hashem, one day before He gave the Torah:

▸ Moshe built a mizbei'ach.

▸ He built 12 stone pillars around the mizbei'ach to represent the 12 shevatim.

---

* Some say that the events at the end of the parashah happened after the Torah was given, and not before. We follow Rashi's commentary on the order of events.

FASCINATING FACTS

The Torah is not a simple history book. Sometimes it tells us about events not in the order that they happened. Something that happened later might be told before something that happened earlier. This is called "ein mukdam u'miuchar baTorah."

For example, the Torah tells us what happened before Mattan Torah in this parashah, instead of in last week's parashah, where it would have been if the Torah were written in order.

———

The laws given non-Jews are called the "Sheva Mitzvos Bnei Noach," The Seven Noachide Laws, because they were given to all of Noach's descendants; all people.

What are the seven laws that Hashem commanded non-Jews to do?

1. Not to worship idols
2. Not to curse Hashem
3. Not to kill another person
4. Not to act in an immoral way
5. Not to steal
6. Set up a system of courts
7. Not to eat a piece of an animal if it was cut off when the animal was alive

- He brought korbanos on the mizbei'ach. The service was done by the firstborn men.

- They gathered the blood of the korbanos in bowls.

- An angel that looked like Moshe came down from heaven and split the blood exactly in half, something no human could do.

- Moshe then sprinkled one half of the blood on the mizbei'ach.

- The Jews listened as Moshe read to them from the Torah he had written the day before, and to the laws that Hashem gave in Marah.

- Then all the Jews together cried out, **"Naaseh v'nishma — Everything that Hashem says we will do and we will listen."**

- Moshe then sprayed the other half of the blood on the people.

- Now the Jews had become Hashem's chosen nation, and we promised to do whatever Hashem tells us to do.

Two Crowns

The Jews didn't say they want to hear what Hashem wants them to do, and then decide if they wanted to do it.

They said: We will do whatever Hashem tells us — no matter what it is. No matter how hard it seems. We are ready to do whatever He says.

There were three million Jews there at Sinai. Not one of them said, "Wait a minute, let me think about it." Not one asked for more information or said, "Sorry, not interested!" They all said: **"We will do and we will listen."**

Such faith and trust deserved a great reward!

Hashem sent down 600,000 angels, each carrying two heavenly crowns. One crown was given because the Jews said "We will do," and the other crown for saying "We will listen." Out of the sky the angels swooped down over the Jews and placed the crowns on their heads.

Hashem's Love

Once again, Moshe, Aharon, Nadav, Avihu, and the seventy wise men went up Har Sinai. There, Hashem showed them a vision so they would know how much He loved the Jews.

They were shown Hashem, with His feet resting on a sapphire-like brick. This meant that all the time the Jews were suffering in Egypt, forced to make bricks, Hashem never forgot them, not even for a second! He kept the brick under His feet to always remind Him of the Jews' pain.

FASCINATING FACTS

When Aharon's sons and the seventy wise men were shown this extremely holy vision, they didn't behave with the proper respect before Hashem's appearance. They ate and drank as if they were at home.

Since Hashem didn't want to cause the Jews any sadness on such a happy day, He didn't punish them then.

Nadav and Avihu died on the day the new Mishkan was ready to be a place where the Jews would serve Hashem. The seventy wise men died when the Jews complained after leaving Har Sinai.

Hashem was always watching and caring for them.

The day after the Jews said "We will do and we will listen," Hashem gave the Aseres HaDibros. (For details on what happened on that unforgettable day, see Parashas Yisro, page 91.)

The Day After

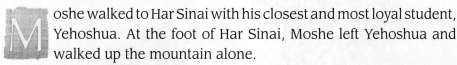

The day after the Aseres HaDibros were given, Hashem called Moshe to come up Har Sinai. From there Hashem would take him up to Shamayim, where Hashem would teach him the Torah. Hashem would also give him the Luchos on which He would write the Aseres HaDibros.

Moshe told the Jewish people he would be gone for 40 days. He told the seventy wise men that Aharon and Chur (his sister Miriam's son) would lead them while he was gone.

The Loyal Student

Moshe walked to Har Sinai with his closest and most loyal student, Yehoshua. At the foot of Har Sinai, Moshe left Yehoshua and walked up the mountain alone.

Yehoshua, the loyal student, didn't move from where Moshe left him. He stayed there all alone, outside the Jewish camp, day and night, waiting for Moshe to come down forty days later. Hashem even sent Yehoshua mahn that fell just for him, right outside his tent, so he wouldn't have to leave.

Moshe Disappears

Moshe climbed the mountain. It looked like there was a fire raging over the mountain, which was also covered by clouds. The Jews below watched their leader get to the top. He went into the cloud and disappeared inside it.

Moshe and the Angels Argue

From the top of Har Sinai Moshe went up to Shamayim. The angels were not happy that Moshe was there to take the Torah from Shamayim to the Jews living on earth. They thought the Torah was too holy to be given to people.

"What is a human being doing up here?" they asked Hashem.

"He came to get the Torah," Hashem answered.

The angels were shocked. "You want to give Your secret, precious treasure to flesh-and-blood people?!" When the angels spoke, fire came out of their mouths.

TORAH IN OUR LIVES

Sometimes we go through hard times. Someone in our family gets sick, or someone starts up with us, or we have a problem in school.

The vision that Hashem showed the wise men is a message to everyone going through a hard time. The message is: Hashem is closest to us when things are hard. He always cares about our pain. He doesn't forget us!

We don't always understand why Hashem lets bad things happen, but He still loves us. He will give us the strength to get through our problems.

WHO'S WHO IN THE TORAH

Yehoshua ben Nun

▸ Yehoshua was from Shevet Ephraim.

▸ He was Moshe's most devoted student.

▸ He led the Jewish army in the war against Amalek.

▸ His real name was Hoshea, but Moshe added the letter "yud" to his name. We will learn about it in Parashas Shelach.

▸ When Moshe died, Yehoshua became the leader of the Jews. He led the Jews into Eretz Yisrael and conquered the land.

▸ Once, during the wars to conquer Eretz Yisrael, Yehoshua told the sun to stop moving in the sky … and it did!

▸ Yehoshua died at the age of 110. He is buried in Kifl Haris, an Arab village in Eretz Yisrael.

"You should answer them," Hashem told Moshe.

"I'm afraid their fire will destroy me," Moshe replied.

"Hold on to My throne," Hashem said, "and answer them."

So began an amazing argument. Moshe tried to persuade the angels that the Torah should be given to humans.

"It says in the Torah that 'I took you out of Egypt,' Moshe told the angels. "Were you slaves in Egypt? Why do you deserve the Torah? And the Torah says not to work on Shabbos, and to rest instead. Do angels work?" Moshe meant: are angels farmers, accountants, teachers or businessmen, who must stop working on Shabbos? "Do angels need rest?" Angels don't need Shabbos!

"The Torah says to honor your father and mother. Angels don't have parents!"

Moshe continued his argument. "Do you have a yetzer hara? Are you ever tempted to do something against the Torah the way people are tempted!?"

Gifts

The angels agreed that Moshe was right and that he should have the Torah. They were so impressed with Moshe and his wisdom that they even gave him gifts.

The Malach HaMaves, the Angel of Death, also gave Moshe a gift. He told Moshe how to stop a plague from killing the Jews. He said that if a plague hits the Jews, Moshe should burn ketores, incense. That would stop the plague. As we will read in Sefer Bamidbar, Moshe actually used this "gift" of the Angel of Death to save Jews from dying in a plague.

Into the Future

When he was in Shamayim, Moshe saw Hashem putting crowns on the letters of the Torah. (These are thin lines that are drawn on top of some of the letters of the Torah.) "What are they for?" he asked.

Hashem explained that one day, there would be a great tzaddik who would explain the many laws that are hidden in the crowns on the Torah letters. That tzaddik would be ... Rabbi Akiva!

Moshe asked to see this tzaddik. Hashem brought Moshe hundreds of years into the future, to Rabbi Akiva's yeshivah. Moshe listened to Rabbi Akiva teach. He realized that Rabbi Akiva was explaining things in a way that he

QUESTIONS, ANYONE?

How long before the world was created did the Torah exist in Shamayim?

974 generations!

___

Non-Jews were given only 7 mitzvos, while the Jews were given 613! Why so many?

Hashem has a special love for us, and wants us to receive a lot of reward for doing these mitzvos. So He gave us 613 opportunities to do good things and earn great reward.

FASCINATING FACTS

The great Rabbi Akiva was a shepherd who did not start learning Torah until he was 40 years old! He started learning, sitting with young children so he could catch up. He went on to become one of the greatest Rabbis and teachers who ever lived! It's never too late to start learning Torah!

did not understand. Moshe felt bad, until he heard Rabbi Akiva tell his students: "What I have taught you are the laws given to Moshe at Har Sinai." When he heard this, Moshe felt better. But he asked Hashem, "Why are You giving the Torah through me? Give it through Rabbi Akiva, who is greater than I am in learning."

Hashem answered, "Quiet. This is My decision."

What's Next?

oshe learned Torah with Hashem for forty days and forty nights. During that time he didn't eat, drink, or sleep.

פָּרָשַׁת
תְּרוּמָה
◆
Parashas
Terumah

Terumah · תְּרוּמָה

Parashah Pointers

▸ Moshe asks the Jews to donate all the materials needed to build the Mishkan. He asks them to bring:

- Gold, silver, and copper
- Wools colored purple, red, and blue
- Linen, goat's hair, skins of rams colored red, and multicolored skins of the "tachash"
- Wood, oil, and spices
- Jewels like diamonds, rubies, sapphires, and others

▸ The Torah explains how to make different parts of the Mishkan:

- אֲרוֹן / **Aron**: The golden box that held the Aseres HaDibros.
- כַּפֹּרֶת / **Kapores**: The cover on top of the Aron. Coming out of it were two golden figures with wings.
- שֻׁלְחָן / **Shulchan**: A table that had the 12 Lechem HaPanim breads on it.
- מְנוֹרָה / **Menorah**: Made of a solid block of gold, the Menorah had seven lamps and many decorations.
- יְרִיעֹת / **Yeri'os**: Three large covers used to cover the Mishkan building.
- קְרָשִׁים / **Kerashim**: Wooden beams covered with gold used to make the walls of the Mishkan.
- אֲדָנִים / **Adanim**: Solid silver bases on which the wooden beams stood. They were the foundation of the Mishkan walls.
- פָּרֹכֶת / **Paroches** and מָסָךְ / **Masach**: Multicolored curtains. The Paroches covered the entrance of the Holy of Holies. The Masach covered the entrance to the Mishkan building.
- מִזְבֵּחַ / **Mizbei'ach**: A tall square box made of wood covered with copper and filled with earth. The korbanos were burned on it. It was located outside the Mishkan building, in the Chatzer, the large Courtyard that surrounded the Mishkan.
- קְלָעִים / **Kela'im**: Linen curtains that enclosed the Chatzer.

Forgiven!

On the first Yom Kippur, about six months after the Jews left Egypt, Moshe came down with the second set of Luchos, the Tablets that contained the Aseres HaDibros. Moshe broke the first ones when he came down from Shamayim carrying them and saw the Jews dancing around the Eigel HaZahav, an idol in the shape of a golden calf. When he saw them doing this terrible sin, Moshe threw the Luchos to the ground, breaking them. (To read more about this, see Parashas Ki Sisa, page 160.)

Hashem gave Moshe the second set of Luchos to show that He forgave the Jews for that terrible sin.

The next day, Moshe told the Jewish people the wonderful news. Hashem wanted them to build a Mishkan. Hashem would rest His Shechinah (His Holy Presence) there and the Jews would bring korbanos.

Our Treasure

The Mishkan would be a place where people could pray to Hashem and bring korbanos. These korbanos would bring down Hashem's blessings on the Jewish people. Thanks to the prayers and korbanos, Hashem would forgive our sins.

The Jews would keep their most precious treasure in the Mishkan — the Luchos.

Tent of Meeting

Another name for the Mishkan was Ohel Moed, the "Tent of Meeting." In a sense, the Mishkan was where the Jews and Hashem would "meet." How? Hashem would speak to Moshe from between the Keruvim, which were on the top of the cover of the Aron. Then Moshe would tell the Jews what Hashem had said.

Donations Please

Moshe asked the Jewish people to donate everything that was needed to build the Mishkan. He also asked them to donate whatever was needed to make the clothing the Kohanim would wear when serving Hashem in the Mishkan.

The Jews immediately went home and started gathering what Moshe asked them to bring. Though Moshe asked for gold, silver, and other expensive items, the Jews brought what Moshe wanted. Giving to the Mishkan was more important than keeping the money for themselves.

Where did all this come from? From the treasures the Jews had taken

QUESTIONS, ANYONE?

Why is the building of the Mishkan discussed in Sefer Shemos? Why isn't it in Sefer Vayikra, which teaches us about all the korbanos brought in the Mishkan?

Sefer Shemos is about the Jews leaving Egypt and getting the Torah. The whole reason the Jews were taken out of Egypt was to receive the Torah and build a place where Hashem's Presence would be here on earth. The mitzvah of building the Mishkan is in Sefer Shemos, because it was one of the reasons for leaving the exile of Egypt!

The tachash existed only at that time so that the Jews could use its beautiful, colorful hide for the Mishkan. It had one horn growing out of the center of its forehead.

QUESTIONS, ANYONE?

What's special about shittim wood?

The letters of the word shittim (שִׁטִּים) are the initials of:
ש-**shalom** — peace
ט-**tovah** — goodness
י-**yeshuah** — help
מ-**mechilah** — forgiveness
These are things we would like Hashem to give us.

out of Egypt. Also, Pharaoh had given his soldiers gold and silver, to bribe them to run after the Jews. When they drowned in the Yam Suf, all these treasures washed up on the beach, and the Jews picked them up. Now, these valuables would become part of the Mishkan and its contents.

MISHKAN BASICS

Any building project begins with the raw materials, things like bricks, wood, and nails.

Moshe asked that the Jews bring the raw materials needed to build the Mishkan. Below is a list of what was needed. It's quite a list.

▸ Gold, silver, copper; wool colored blue, purple, and red. Linen, goat's hair, skins of rams colored red, "tachash" skin, shittim wood, precious stones, oil, and spices.

▸ **Techeiles, which is dyed a shade of blue.** *
Techeiles was made by dipping the wool into the blood of the chilazon, a snail-like creature that lives in the sea.

▸ **The many-colored skins of the tachash animal.** Never heard of a tachash? That's because Hashem created it just for the building of the Mishkan. It doesn't exist anymore.

▸ **Wood from a tree called shittim.** There are no trees in the desert, so from where did the Jews get shittim wood? Yaakov Avinu brought the trees with him when he went to Egypt, and he planted them there. Yaakov told his children that when they leave Egypt they should take the trees with them. They would need them to build the Mishkan.

▸ **Oil for the Menorah.** This oil was made from the very best olives — the ones picked from the top of the tree — which were then gently crushed. The first oil that came out was the purest and best oil.

▸ **Different-smelling spices.** Some spices were mixed with oil and smeared on the head of the first Kohanim, of a Kohen when he became the Kohen Gadol, and also on a new Jewish king. The mixture of oil and spices was also smeared on the Mishkan building itself, and everything that was inside it, to make them holy. Other spices, eleven of them, were mixed to make the Ketores, a sweet-smelling incense, which was burned every day on the Golden Mizbei'ach.

▸ **Jewels** like diamonds, rubies, sapphires and others, that were used for the Kohen Gadol's special garments. They were donated by the nesi'im, princes of the shevatim. These stones came straight from heaven! When the mahn fell every morning, pearls and jewels rained down as well.

* There are opinions that techeiles is wool colored sea-green.

THE ARON
Torah First / Aron First

Now the parashah gives us all the details of exactly how to build the Mishkan, and how to make the items that will be in it.

The Torah starts by teaching us about the Aron — the box that will hold the Luchos. That makes sense, since the Torah is the most important. The Torah was created even before the world. First, Hashem taught Moshe how to make the Aron, because the Aron is the holiest object in the Mishkan. It was placed in a room just by itself. The room was called the Kodesh HaKodashim (Holy of Holies).

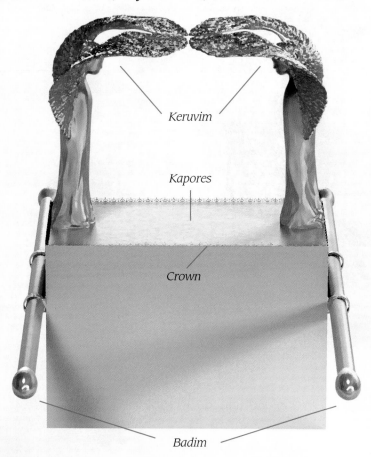

Keruvim

Kapores

Crown

Badim

TORAH IN OUR LIVES

The Jews used some of the gold they had collected at the Yam Suf to make the Eigel HaZahav (see page 160). That meant they used a gift Hashem gave them for a sin. Now the Jews were doing teshuvah for their sin by giving gold they collected at the Yam Suf to do a mitzvah — to build the Mishkan.

The Mishkan was built as a way for us to make up for the terrible sin of the Eigel HaZahav. It was "shtus," the Hebrew word for "stupidity," to make the Eigel HaZahav. The word shtus in Hebrew sounds like the word "shittim," which is the kind of wood used to build the Mishkan. The Jews were saying: We want to do a mitzvah through "shittim" instead of an aveirah through "shtus."

They gave their gold to build the Eigel HaZahav. They would now be going to give their gold for a mitzvah — building the Mishkan.

From this we can learn how to behave if we sinned.

Did you insult or even hurt someone's feelings? Make up for it. Apologize and go out of your way to become his friend.

You didn't throw out the garbage when you were asked to do so? Make up for it, offer to do it when you weren't asked.

All for Torah

Hashem told Moshe that all the Jews should take part in building the Aron. Everyone should give a small piece of gold that would be used in making it, or should somehow help in making the Aron. That way everyone will have a connection to the Luchos, which are in the Aron.

Every Jew has a share in the Torah. If someone can't study Gemara, he can study Mishnah or Chumash or Halachah (Jewish law). Someone who finds it very hard to study can support yeshivos and people who study Torah. Torah is for everyone!

Measurements: The Torah teaches us the size of everything in the Mishkan. It uses measurements called "amos" and "tefachim." There are different opinions of what a tefach and an amah are in inches and feet.

In this book we define a tefach as approximately 4 inches and an amah as approximately 2 feet. Just remember these are not exact numbers.

Gold is very expensive! Why cover the inside of the Aron with gold, if no one sees it anyway?

Covering the inside with gold teaches us that we have to be "gold" inside as well as outside. Someone who just acts like a Torah scholar, trying to impress people, but in his heart is really not sincere, is not a true Torah scholar.

Shittim Wood and Solid Gold

The Aron was made of three boxes. The main one was made of shittim wood and the other two were made of gold. One of the gold boxes was a bit bigger than the wooden box and the other gold box was a bit smaller than the wooden box. The wooden box was put into the bigger golden box and the smaller golden box was put inside the wooden one, so all the wood was covered with gold.

After the three boxes were put one inside the other, if you were looking at the top you would still see the top of the wooden box in between the gold. To cover that, a thin piece of gold was placed on top of the boxes. Now, no matter from what direction you looked, you would see only gold.

FASCINATING FACTS

Do you like wearing gold jewelry? Thank the Mishkan and Beis HaMikdash! If it wasn't that gold was needed to build them, Hashem wouldn't have created it! Gold was created only for that reason.

Wood?

Why wasn't the Aron made of one box of gold? What is G-d's message when He instructs us to place a box of wood between the gold boxes?

There are many answers. Here are a few:

▸ To remind us that the Torah is the tree of life. You want to have a good life? Live according to the Torah's rules. Be like a tree that grows. Never stop learning Torah, keep growing in Torah knowledge.

▸ A wooden box isn't worth much, but if it's carrying the Torah, we cover it with gold boxes. When something is enclosed in gold boxes, we know it's very valuable. This teaches us how much we must honor and respect scholars, even if they are poor. The Torah inside them is like the wood of the Aron, deserving to be covered with gold.

▸ The wooden box reminds us that Torah study is like a tree that grows fruit. The fruits of Torah study are the rewards that grow in Heaven. They will be enjoyed by those who study Torah. (Of course, that's besides the rewards they will get in this world.)

The Golden Crown

The outer gold box of the Aron, the one that could be seen, was higher than the other boxes and had a decoration all around its top. When all the parts of the Aron were put together it looked like there was a crown on the Aron.

The Angels

Every box needs a cover. The cover of the Aron was called the Kapores and it was made of solid gold. At each end of the cover were statues of angels, called Keruvim, about 40 inches high. One had the face of a boy, and the other had the face of a girl. Reaching out to each other over their heads were their wings. The wings stretched out up above the Aron, like an umbrella.

Hugging Angels

On the holidays of Pesach, Shavuos, and Succos the curtains of the Kodesh HaKodashim were opened, and the Jews were shown the Aron. They would see a miracle! The two Keruvim, which were at opposite ends of the Aron cover, miraculously moved together and hugged each other. This was a symbol of Hashem's love for the Jewish people.

Rings and Poles

Attached to the Aron were four golden rings, one on each of the narrower sides of the Aron, at the corners. The poles of the Aron, called the Badim, were put through the rings. The poles were made of wood covered with gold.

QUESTIONS, ANYONE?

Why were the faces on the Keruvim the faces of children?

To teach how precious the Torah learned by children is to Hashem. Also, to show parents the importance of teaching their young children Torah and mitzvos.

FASCINATING FACTS

The Keruvim faced each other, so they would look like two friends studying Torah together.

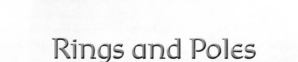

QUESTIONS, ANYONE?

Though other items in the Mishkan, like the Shulchan and Mizbei'ach, also had poles, the Aron's poles were different. They were thicker at each end than the rest of the pole. Why was that?

The poles for the Shulchan and Mizbei'ach were designed to carry them while traveling from place to place. Once the Jews arrived at the new location and put together the Mishkan, the poles were removed. But not those of the Aron. Its poles stayed in their rings all the time. The tips of the poles were thicker than the rest of the pole, so pulling them out of the narrow rings would be hard. This reminded those who carried the Mishkan not to remove them!

We all know that we have to honor someone who knows a lot of Torah, a talmid chacham. What if he becomes ill and forgets his learning — do we still have to honor him?

Yes. We know this because the Luchos that Moshe broke were kept in the Aron along with the unbroken Luchos. Though a talmid chacham is sick and broken, we still honor him, even if he can't learn anymore.

Moshe's Torah

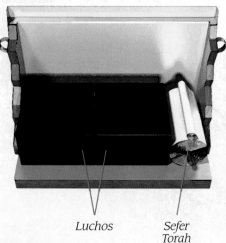

Luchos   Sefer Torah

The Aron was built to hold the Aseres HaDibros that Moshe brought down from Har Sinai. The Sefer Torah that he wrote was also put into the Aron.

Hidden Treasure

Where is the Aron today? There are three opinions! Rabbi Eliezer says it was taken to Babylonia when the First Beis HaMikdash was destroyed.

Rabbi Yehudah says it was hidden during the time of the First Beis HaMikdash under its original place in the Kodesh HaKodashim.

Other Rabbis say it was hidden away on the Temple Mount, under the room where they checked the wood to be burned on the Mizbei'ach.

Hot Bread

Every Shabbos the Kohanim would enter the Mishkan with 12 loaves of bread. These loaves, which were not chametz, were called Lechem HaPanim. They would be put on the Shulchan (Table). Kohanim removed the bread that had been on the racks since the previous Shabbos, and, at the same time, put the new ones in place.

Miraculously, the week-old bread was still hot when it was taken off the Shulchan! It felt as if it had just come out of the oven, instead of a week before.

After the bread was removed, it was divided among the Kohanim. The bread was very special. A Kohen who ate only a small amount of it would be full, as if he had eaten an entire meal.

THE SHULCHAN (TABLE)

The Shulchan was made of shittim wood, rectangular in shape and covered in gold. Around its top was a decoration, making it look as if the table had a crown. Gold rings were attached to the corners at the top of the table legs. When traveling, gold-covered wooden poles were placed in the rings. The Levi'im used them to lift and carry the Shulchan.

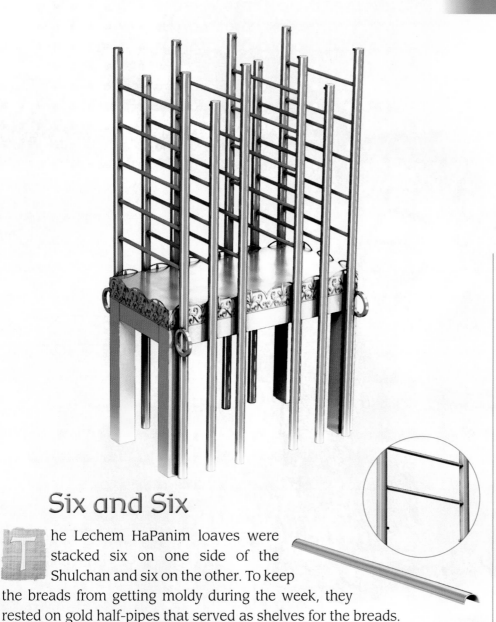

Six and Six

The Lechem HaPanim loaves were stacked six on one side of the Shulchan and six on the other. To keep the breads from getting moldy during the week, they rested on gold half-pipes that served as shelves for the breads.

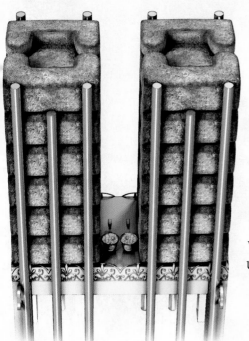

What kept the pipes up? Twelve gold poles were connected to the Shulchan. They rested on the floor and rose high up over the Shulchan. The half-pipes rested on the pegs coming out of the poles. One end of a half-pipe rested on one peg and the other end on the peg directly opposite. This created metal shelves for the breads to rest on.

One loaf rested directly on the Shulchan and the other five rested on the pipes. Looking at the Shulchan, you would see two towers of loaves stacked up on the Shulchan.

TORAH IN OUR LIVES

Everything in the Torah has something to teach us. For example, here is something we can learn from the measurements of the Shulchan. It was two amos long by one amah wide. These are whole numbers, not fractions.

The Shulchan is a symbol of wealth, of making a living. The whole numbers of the Shulchan hint to us to be happy with as much as Hashem gives us. We should feel that what we have is enough. We shouldn't feel bad just because we don't have the latest device or designer clothing, or more money. Whatever Hashem gives us is all we need. We are whole. Nothing is missing.

On the other hand ... the height of the Shulchan is a fraction. It is 1½ amos high. Why? People who become rich sometimes think of themselves as being better, higher than others. The height of the Shulchan is a "broken" number, to remind the rich that even though they may be "high" they are still only "half" and they should be humble.

In the time of the Second Beis HaMikdash there was only one family that knew the secret of making the Lechem HaPanim. No one else was able to bake the loaves in a way that the dough would hold its shape when it came out of the oven. The family's name is recorded in the Gemara for us to remember forever. The name was Garmu.

The Torah lists all the parts and items needed to make the Shulchan. The last one mentioned are the Menakiyos, pipes that supported the breads.

The word Menakiyos sounds like the Hebrew word "naki," which means "clean." This hints that the money we make, to put food on our table, should be "clean" of sin — that is, it should be earned honestly.

Bread with "Horns"

The Lechem HaPanim had a very unique shape. It had a flat bottom, with two raised sides. Extra pieces of dough, called "horns," were attached to the two raised sides.

The breads were baked in an iron baking pan that had the same shape they had. When the loaves were taken out of the oven, the hot breads were put on gold pans. There they stayed until it was time to put them on the Shulchan.

Gold Spoons

On Shabbos, when 12 fresh loaves were put on the Shulchan, two golden spoons of levonah, frankincense (a spice), were put there as well. These spoons were kept on the Shulchan all week. When the next Shabbos came and the old Lechem HaPanim were removed from the Shulchan, these spoons were removed as well and replaced with other spoons with fresh levonah. The old levonah was thrown into the fires on the Mizbei'ach.

THE MENORAH

Seven Lights

Every day Aharon, the Kohen Gadol, lit the Menorah in the Mishkan in the late afternoon. The lamps stayed lit throughout the night. The Menorah in the Mishkan had seven lights.

A Block of Gold

To make the Menorah, Moshe started with a block of gold. Hashem showed Moshe what the Menorah should look like. The Menorah had to be formed out of one huge golden block. But it was simply too hard for a person to make. So Hashem told Moshe, "Throw the gold into the fire." Hashem made a miracle and out of the fire came a beautiful gold Menorah, exactly the way Hashem had showed Moshe it should look.

There are two opinions about how the Menorah's branches were shaped.

FASCINATING FACTS

The Menorah is a symbol of Torah. Its 22 decorative cups stand for the 22 letters of the aleph-beis, the letters with which the Torah is written.

Six Feet High

The Menorah was about 3 amos (six feet) high, the height of a tall adult. It had seven bowls at the top. The best quality olive oil (made from the first drops pressed from the best olives of each picking) was poured into each bowl, and wicks were added.

It had six gracefully curving branches* coming out of a tall center branch, three on each side. At the bottom of the center branch was a three-legged square base.

A Great Life

Torah is always compared to light. The Menorah's lights represent Torah wisdom, and those who study it. The Torah lights up our lives by giving us wisdom and understanding, so we can understand what Hashem wants of us. That's the secret of a great life.

Decorations

Of all the items in the Mishkan, the one that had the most decorations on it was the Menorah. The Torah gives us instructions about what these decorations should look like and where they should be.

---

* There is an opinion that the branches were straight and rose up on a slant.

The Adanim were the base for the Mishkan's walls. The silver for the Adanim came from the half-shekel that each Jew had to contribute to the Mishkan. This means that the base that held up the Mishkan came from all the Jews, and everyone gave the same amount.

Here's something we can learn from this: When Jews are working together, and when no Jew feels he is better than the others — that's how we bring Hashem close to us.

So you have a choice. You can think you're better than another kid in your class because you're smarter or more popular, or you can play ball better or paint a prettier picture. So you won't be that kid's friend. Or you can reach out in friendship to another Jew, and feel Hashem's closeness. The choice is yours.

There were three kinds of decorations:

- ▸ **Geivi'im:** These were shaped like cups. There were 22 of them on the Menorah.

- ▸ **Kaftorim:** These were ball-shaped decorations. There were 11 of them.

- ▸ **Perachim:** Rose-petal-shaped flowers. There were 9 of them.

Even the decorations had decorations! There were small almond-shaped designs on each of these decorations.

Location

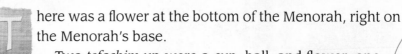

There was a flower at the bottom of the Menorah, right on the Menorah's base.

Two *tefachim* up were a cup, ball, and flower, one inside the other.

Two *tefachim* higher was a ball. Two of the Menorah's branches came out of this ball, one on the right and one on the left.

One *tefach* higher was another ball. The next two of the Menorah's branches came out of this ball, one on the right and one on the left.

At the top of each of the Menorah's seven branches were three cups, one ball, and one flower, and a bowl into which the oil was poured.

THE MISHKAN WALLS

Building Beams

The shittim trees that Yaakov had planted in Egypt became the walls of the Mishkan.

The trees were cut into Kerashim, which were rectangular beams 10 amos (20 feet) high and 1½ amos (3 feet) wide. They were covered with gold plate. Two thick pegs stuck out from the bottom of each beam. In the center of each beam was a small hole that went through from one side to the other. A long stick, called Briach, was put through the center holes of all the beams. This helped keep all the Kerashim together in place, as we will see later.

The pegs on the base of the beam fit into the Adanim. The Adanim were solid blocks of silver that had a hole in the center for a peg to fit into. Each beam was held in place by two Adanim.

The Building

The Mishkan building was in the shape of a rectangle. It had three walls made of the Kerashim. The fourth side was left open to be used as the entrance.

To assemble the Mishkan walls, the Levi'im placed 40 Adanim in a straight line and then fitted twenty Kerashim on top of the Adanim. They did the same for the other side.

There were now two walls, one on the right facing north, and one on the left facing south. In between the two walls, to make the back wall, they laid out 16 Adanim and fitted in 8 Kerashim. This wall was in the west.

Right Side Up

If someone shakes the lulav, but holds it upside down — has he performed the mitzvah? The answer is no, because the lulav has to be held in the direction that it grew.

How do we know that mitzvos have to be done right side up? We learn it from the beams of the Mishkan. Hashem gave strict instructions: When the beams are put up, they should be put in the direction they grew. The part of the beam that had come from the bottom of the tree is at the bottom of the Mishkan.

This rule applies to all the mitzvos.

Keeping the Walls Steady and Strong

Tabaos were hollow gold rectangles that fit into slits cut into the top of each Keresh. These Tabaos held the Kerashim tightly together and helped keep the wall stable.

To make the walls even stronger they did the following:

Five feet from the top and bottom of each beam were gold rings and two half-pipes, one on each side of the ring.

When all the beams were put together it looked like there was a gold pipe running across the back of the wall near the top, and another one near the bottom. Then they put wooden poles through the gold pipes and rings, on the top and bottom.

FASCINATING FACTS

The wood used in the Mishkan, a building built for Hashem, did not come from fruit trees. We learn from this that when we build our homes we should not use fruit trees either.

Cutting down fruit trees to use their wood for building is a waste. Why destroy a tree that can grow food and feed people, when you can use a tree that has no fruits?

Tabaos

Half-pipes

The Pole that Bends

Take a straight wooden pole and try to bend it. It is impossible. Yet running through the center hole of all the beams of the Mishkan walls was one long amazing beam.

It went through the northern wall and when it reached the western wall it **bent**. It passed through the western wall. When it reached the southern wall, it **bent again**! It passed through the beams of the southern wall.

This miracle happened many times — every time they took apart the Mishkan, and again when they put it back up. Each time they put the pole in, it bent again.

The Entrance

In front of the Mishkan building was the Masach, a multicolored curtain. It hung on five wooden beams covered in gold. These beams were supported by copper, and they had a gold cord wrapped around them.

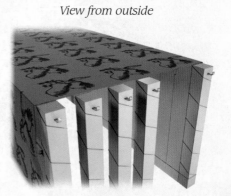

View from inside　　*Beams*　　*View from outside*

THE KODESH HAKODASHIM — HOLY OF HOLIES

Only on Yom Kippur

The Aron stood in the most important part of the Mishkan building — the back section called the Kodesh HaKodashim, Holy of Holies. This room, which was 10 amos by 10 amos (20 feet by 20 feet), was so holy that no one was allowed to enter it, except on Yom Kippur, the holiest day of the year. Even then, only the Kohen Gadol was allowed in.

It was separated from the front section of the Mishkan by a multicolored curtain called the Paroches. The Paroches hung on four gold-covered wooden beams. Each one rested on one silver Aden (base).

Jar, Stick, and Oil

esides the Aron there were other objects placed in the Kodesh HaKodashim:

▸ A jar of mahn, the food that fell from heaven to feed the Jews in the desert.

▸ The walking stick of Aharon, which miraculously sprouted almond blossoms at the time of Korach's rebellion.

▸ The Shemen HaMishchah (Anointing Oil) used to anoint the kings and the Kohen Gadol.

THE KODESH

Left, Right, Middle

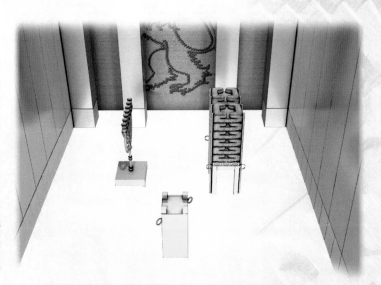

he front section of the Mishkan building was called the Kodesh. In it were the Shulchan, Menorah, and the small Golden Mizbei'ach (this Mizbei'ach is discussed in the next parashah; see page 152).

When entering the Kodesh, the small Golden Mizbei'ach stood 10 amos from the entrance, in the middle of the room. The Shulchan and the Menorah were further into the room, 5 amos (10 feet) from the Kodesh HaKodashim, with the Shulchan on the right side and the Menorah on the left.

Golden Crowns

he Aron, the Shulchan, and the small Mizbei'ach all had a gold band around the top looking like a crown. Why just these?

Each crown stood for a different type of leadership that we Jews have.

▸ The Torah is royalty. The crown on the Aron stands for anyone who studies Torah. This is the crown of the Torah leaders. And this is the crown that anyone can earn. It doesn't make a difference what family they come from, it doesn't make a difference how rich or how poor they are. The crown of Torah, the crown on the Aron, can be earned by anyone who dedicates himself to Torah learning.

▸ The crown of the Shulchan stands for the royal line of King David. The Shulchan, piled high with bread, symbolized food and prosperity. The king is the nation's leader, and he is responsible for the nation's economy and for making the people prosperous.

▸ The crown of the Golden Mizbei'ach, which stood in a place where only Kohanim were allowed to enter, stands for the royal line of Kohanim, Aharon's children. Only they were allowed to perform the services in the Heichal (Mishkan building) and burn Ketores on the Golden Mizbei'ach.

THE YERI'OS (COVERINGS)

The roof of the Mishkan was made of Yeri'os. There were three Yeri'os. The lowest one is what you would see if you were in the Mishkan looking up, its ceiling. It was made of a multicolored cloth material. The second, sandwiched in between the bottom and top Yeri'os, was made of goat hair. The third, which was on top, was made of red-dyed ram skins and the multicolored skin of the tachash animal.

Traveling Tent

The Mishkan was like a tent.

Have you ever gone camping? In the morning you take down your tent, fold it up, and take it with you to the next place. As the Jews traveled through the desert, the Mishkan would be taken apart and rebuilt later, at their next stop.

When the Jews moved, the Yeri'os were taken down and folded.

The Ceiling

Ten pieces of multicolored cloth were made. Each one looked like a very long scarf. They were 28 amos (56 feet) long and 4 amos (8 feet) wide.

Then five of these pieces were sewn together, and the other five were sewn together as well. You now had two large pieces of cloth, each one 28x20 amos. That's wider than many homes!

The two large pieces were laid side by side. To connect them, they used 50 gold hooks and 50 loops that had been sewn onto the two large cloths. (Imagine buttoning a shirt with golden hooks instead of buttons!) The entire cloth was placed over the Mishkan.

The Ten Strips

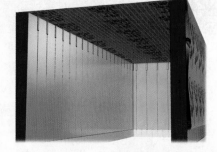

This seems to be a strange way to make the Mishkan ceiling. Why not just make one large piece of cloth to put over the Mishkan? Why make it in ten strips? If you are going to make it in ten strips, why not sew all the strips together instead of sewing them five and five and then connecting them with hooks and loops? The cover of the Mishkan was made to resemble the Aseres HaDibros. They appeared on the Luchos with five commandments on one stone and five on the other. So five strips of cloth were sewn together into one half, and five strips were sewn together for the second half.

And the hooks? There were fifty of them, to remind us that there are fifty levels of binah, understanding, in which the Torah can be understood.

The Middle Cover

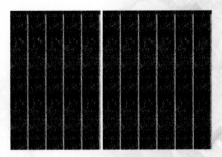

Over the cloth ceiling there was another cloth, this one made of goat hair.

Eleven long strips of goat hair were made, each one 30 amos (60 feet) long and 4 amos (8 feet) wide.

They then sewed five strips together and six strips together. The two large pieces made of goat hair were then put side by side and connected with 50 copper hooks inserted into loops that had been sewn on.

The large goat-hair cover was put over the ceiling cloth. It hung down the sides of the walls of the Mishkan. When you looked at the Mishkan you could see it covering the walls.

On Top

Half of the top cover was made from the skin of the tachash and half from red-dyed ram skins. It was 10 amos (20 feet) by 30 amos (60 feet). Unlike the other covers, this one didn't hang down over the Mishkan walls at all; it covered just the top of the inside of the Mishkan.

THE COPPER MIZBEI'ACH

Fire and Smoke

This Mizbei'ach was where most of the service in the Mishkan was performed. It was through the services done on this Mizbei'ach that the Jews were forgiven for their sins.

Fires were always burning on it. The smoke would rise in a straight pillar that could be seen by all the Jews camped around the Mishkan.

On the Mizbei'ach they burned the korbanos of individual Jews. They also burned the communal korbanos of the Jewish nation, like the daily morning and afternoon korbanos and the special korbanos brought on Shabbos and Jewish holidays.

Three Miracles of the Mizbei'ach

Every day, miracles happened.

1. No matter how windy it was, the smoke rose up in a straight column.
2. No matter how hard it rained ... the fire never went out!
3. Even though the Mizbei'ach was made of wood, with only a thin layer of copper, it never caught fire.

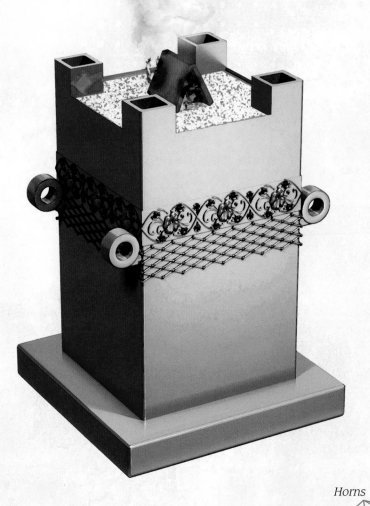

FASCINATING FACTS

The letters of the word Mizbei'ach (מִזְבֵּחַ) are the initials of:

מ·**mechilah** — forgiveness

ז·**zechus** — merit

ב·**berachah** — blessing

ח·**chaim** — long life

These words show the power of the Mizbei'ach and what it did for the Jewish people.

Hollow

The Mizbei'ach stood about 10 amos (20 feet) high and was made of shittim wood covered with copper. It was shaped like a tall box that was empty on the inside. The inside was filled with earth until the top. It was on the earth that the fires of the Mizbei'ach burned.

In front of the Mizbei'ach was a long ramp that the Kohanim used to walk up to the top.

Horns

The Mizbei'ach stood on a square base — the Yesod. Rising above the top of the Mizbei'ach, at each corner, were "horns." These were small square boxes 5 tefachim (20 inches) high.

Fish Netting and Flowers

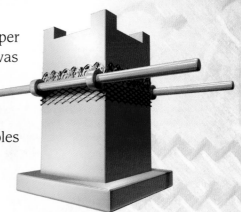

Right above the middle of the Mizbei'ach were decorative copper bands, like copper belts, wrapped all the way around. One was called the Michbar, and it looked like fishing net. On top of the Michbar was the Karkov. It was a band of copper that had flowers engraved on it.

How was the Mizbei'ach carried when they journeyed? Wooden poles were covered with copper and put into copper rings attached to the Michbar.

Trapped!

Fishermen use nets to trap fish. They will put some fish food in the net for bait, then put the net into the water. When the fish come to eat, they close the net around them. The fish are trapped!

The yetzer hara works the same way. We don't want to sin. But the yetzer hara sets his trap. He puts bait in front of us and we want to take it, even though we know we shouldn't.

Here's an example. You see something really foolish that your brother did. What a great story — all your friends will laugh. You want to tell them all about it!

Your friends' laughter, and the feeling you get from being popular with them — that's the yetzer hara's bait. If you take the bait and speak badly of your brother — you've gotten trapped in its net! If you hold yourself back and don't tell anyone — you are one smart fish who didn't take the bait.

That's one of the reasons why there was a Michbar on the Mizbei'ach. The Michbar looked like a fish net. When people who sinned would come to the Mishkan and bring korbanos, to be forgiven for their sins, they would see the net. This would save them from the yetzer hara's net in the future.

THE CHATZER (COURTYARD)
Curtains

The area on which the main building of the Mishkan and the Mizbei'ach stood was called the Chatzer. It was large, 100 amos (200 feet) long and 50 amos (100 feet) wide. Anyone who was tamei could not enter this area.

The Chatzer was surrounded by Kela'im, a wall of pure white linen curtains hanging on wooden beams covered with copper. At the bottom of each beam was one peg. The peg fitted into a copper Aden (base). In order to keep the curtains from blowing in the wind, the curtains were tied to copper pegs hammered into the ground.

Silver Strings and Caps

ach beam of the Chatzer was topped with a silver cap. Silver cords were wound around the beam.

Different

he eastern wall was a bit different than the others, because that was where the Jews entered the Chatzer. Three beams were put up on one side of the entrance and three on the other. The linen curtains were stretched and hung over these beams, leaving an entranceway in the middle.

In front of the entranceway four more beams were put up. On these were hung the Masach, a multicolored curtain. When people wanted to go in, the curtain was pushed aside.

Stats

he Torah gives us the exact measurements of the Mishkan complex and the items inside it.*

Here they are:

אֲרוֹן /Aron (Ark)	2.5 amos long x 1.5 amos wide x 1.5 amos high (60 inches x 36 inches x 36 inches)
שֻׁלְחָן / Shulchan (Table)	2 amos long x 1 amah wide x 1.5 amos high (48 inches x 24 inches x 36 inches)
מְנוֹרָה / Menorah	3 amos high (72 inches)
מִזְבֵּחַ / Mizbei'ach (Altar)	5 amos long x 5 amos wide x 10 amos high (10 feet x 10 feet x 20 feet)
Mishkan building	30 amos long x 10 amos wide x 10 amos high (60 feet x 20 feet x 20 feet)
Entire area of Mishkan complex	100 amos long x 50 amos wide (200 feet x 100 feet)

There are different opinions as to the size of an amah. This chart was made using Rabbi Meir's opinion that there are six tefachim (handbreadths) to an amah. Because of the differences of opinions about the size of an amah in inches we have rounded it off to one amah=2 feet.

פָּרָשַׁת
תְּצַוֶּה
◆
Parashas
Tetzaveh

Tetzaveh · תְּצַוֶּה

Parashah Pointers

▸ The Torah tells us how the Menorah in the Mishkan should be lit.

▸ Aharon and his sons and their descendants are chosen to be the Kohanim. They will perform the service in the Mishkan (and, centuries later, in the Beis HaMikdash).

▸ Hashem instructs how the Bigdei Kehunah, the clothing of the Kohanim, should be made.

▸ **The Kohen Gadol's clothing:**

- אֵפֹד / **Ephod**: This looked like an apron with two shoulder straps. There was a precious stone on the shoulder of each strap.

- חֹשֶׁן / **Choshen**: Worn on the Kohen Gadol's chest, it had 12 precious gems on it.

- מְעִיל / **Me'il**: A long blue shirt.

- צִיץ / **Tzitz**: A gold plate the Kohen Gadol wore on his forehead. On it were the words, "Kodesh LaHashem — Holy to Hashem."

▸ **Clothing worn by both the Kohen Gadol and the Kohen Hedyot (an "ordinary" Kohen):**

- מִכְנָסַיִם / **Michnasayim**: Short pants worn under the Kohen's clothing.

- כֻּתֹּנֶת / **Kutones**: A long shirt that covered his body down to his heels.

- אַבְנֵט / **Avnet**: A long wide belt wrapped around his waist.

- מִגְבָּעַת, מִצְנֶפֶת / **Migbaas** (for the Kohen Hedyot), **Mitznefes** (for the Kohen Gadol): A hat that was worn like a turban. The Kohen was given a long narrow piece of linen cloth that was wrapped around his head.

▸ The Torah teaches which mitzvos Moshe should do for seven days, in order to prepare the Mishkan. Those seven days will also give Aharon and his sons the holiness to serve in the Mishkan.

▸ The procedures needed to make the Copper Mizbei'ach holy are discussed.

▸ The mitzvah to bring the Korban Tamid, an offering brought every morning and every afternoon, is discussed.

▸ Mizbach HaKetores/Incense Altar: The Torah describes how to build the gold-covered Mizbei'ach to burn Ketores, spices, every day. It is also called the Mizbach HaZahav.

The Missing Name

T here is something missing in this parashah. It's one word, and it's a name.

The missing name is Moshe.

From when we read about his birth in Parashas Shemos, until the last parashah in the Torah, Moshe is always mentioned. But not in this parashah. Look at every page, every pasuk — no Moshe. Why?

When the Jews sinned with the Eigel HaZahav, Moshe begged Hashem to forgive them. At one point, Moshe said if Hashem wouldn't forgive them, He should erase Moshe's name from the Torah.

Of course, Hashem forgave them. But because the words of a tzaddik are very powerful, once Moshe said his name should be taken out of the Torah, it had to happen. So Hashem took his name out of one of the parshiyos of the Torah. This one.

THE MENORAH

Pure Light

T he Jews were told to use only the purest olive oil to light the Menorah.

They picked the best olives, the ones that grow on top of the tree, where they get the most sunlight. Then they gently crushed the olives. Only the first drops that came out were used for the Menorah.

Each day, in the late afternoon, the seven cups of the Menorah were filled with half a *log* (about 10 ounces) of oil. The Menorah had to stay lit all night. That was enough to last through the longest nights of the winter, so they used that amount for all the days of the year.

Wicks

T he wicks were put in the cups so that they all faced the middle flame. The wick of the middle cup stood straight up.

The Light that Never Went Out

B y morning, all the Menorah's flames had gone out — except the middle one. Though there was only enough oil in each of the cups to last one night, miraculously, that middle flame kept burning all day! This daily miracle reminded the Jews how much Hashem loves us and how close He is to us. He loves us so much He made this miracle every single day.

QUESTIONS, ANYONE?

Though Moshe is mentioned in many parshiyos, there are some parshiyos in Sefer Devarim where he is not mentioned by name. Why is that?

Because, as you will find out when we reach Sefer Devarim, in Devarim Moshe is doing the talking. His name doesn't have to be mentioned — the words are his words!

FASCINATING FACTS

What a tzaddik says often happens, because the mouth of a tzaddik is holy. He uses his mouth mostly for Torah study and prayer. A tzaddik doesn't say bad things about other people, and he doesn't use his mouth to hurt anyone with his words. So when a tzaddik speaks — Hashem listens! That is why people go to a tzaddik for a blessing — for good health, children, livelihood and any other need. They are hoping that when the tzaddik blesses them, Hashem will make those blessings come true.

The word כָּתִית (crushed) contains a hidden message! It tells the Jews how long the Menorah would remain lit during the time of the First and Second Batei Mikdash, before they would be destroyed. The Second Beis HaMikdash stood for 420 years — the number value of the first two letters in the word: כת. The First Beis HaMikdash was standing for 410 years, the number value of the next two letters in the word: ית

We can learn from the way the Menorah was lit what a teacher has to do. A teacher should "light up" a love for Torah and mitzvos in the students. Teachers should make sure that the students have a blazing flame of love for Hashem, His Torah, and mitzvos.

Aharon was the great peacemaker of the Jewish people. When people were angry with each other, or if a husband and wife weren't getting along, Aharon was the one who made peace between them. It's hard to get angry people to forgive each other, but Aharon had the wisdom and talent to do it.

If the Jews committed a sin, the prayers and services of the Mishkan would help make peace between Hashem and His people. Who could be a better choice for the job of serving in the Mishkan than Aharon, the great peacemaker? With Aharon and his descendants in charge, Hashem knew that they would do their very best to get Him to forgive His people.

So next time you see two of your friends or your siblings fighting — try to make peace between them. It's what Hashem wants and as a bonus, your reward will be very great!

Even though the Kohen could have let the middle flame keep burning all the time, Hashem gave a mitzvah to light *all* the Menorah's cups every day. Some opinions say that the Kohen would blow out the middle flame every day in the afternoon and then light it again. Others say he would just reset it by adding more oil.

Sputter, Sputter

It wouldn't look nice if while the Kohen was lighting one wick, another wick would sputter and go out. So Hashem said that the Kohen who lights the Menorah should make sure that the wick he is lighting is burning with a strong flame before he moves on to the next wick.

THE KOHANIM AND THEIR CLOTHING

Kohanim

Hashem chose Aharon and his sons — Nadav, Avihu, Elazar, and Issamar — to be the Kohanim. Only they and their children would be allowed to do the holy work in the Mishkan and Beis HaMikdash.

Special Clothes

A Kohen couldn't just walk in off the street and start working in the Mishkan dressed in weekday clothes. Not even in Shabbos clothes.

Hashem told Moshe to have the Jews make four special articles of clothing for the Kohen Hedyot, the "ordinary" Kohen, to wear. These are called "Bigdei Kehunah." He was allowed to work in the Mishkan only when wearing these special clothes.

The greatest of all the Kohanim, the Kohen Gadol, wore eight special pieces of clothing, four more than the ordinary Kohen.

THE KOHEN GADOL

The Golden Clothing

The Kohen Gadol's Bigdei Kehunah are called the "Bigdei Zahav" because his extra four pieces of clothing all had some gold in them.

This is how they were made:

Ephod / Apron

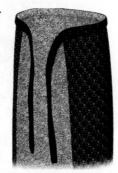

The Ephod looked like an apron. But instead of covering his front, the Ephod covered the Kohen Gadol's back. It reached down from his waist, all the way to his heels.

He would tie the Ephod around his waist right below his elbows with the straps that came out of its top edge. The Ephod was wide enough that it came around the front of his body, covering his hips and sides.

The Shoulder Straps

Sewn onto the top edge of the Ephod were shoulder straps. The straps came up over the Kohen Gadol's shoulders and reached his chest.

The straps and the Ephod were made of multicolored cloth that had gold threads running through it.

12 Shevatim

Two hollow golden boxes were attached to the place where the shoulder straps covered the Kohen Gadol's shoulder. Each of the two hollow golden boxes was deep enough to hold a precious stone.

Two precious stones, called Shoham stones, were placed inside the boxes, one on each shoulder strap. Carved into the stones were the names of the 12 shevatim in the order they were born.

The Kohen Gadol wore the names of six shevatim — Reuven, Shimon, Levi, Yehudah, Dan, and Naftali — on one shoulder. On the other shoulder were the names of the other six — Gad, Asher, Yissachar, Zevulun, Yosef, and Binyamin.

The Choshen / Breastplate

On the Kohen Gadol's chest was the Choshen. It was a piece of multicolored cloth, one amah long and a half-amah wide (about 2 feet by 1 foot). The piece of cloth was folded over to make a square, one half-amah by one half-amah. The inside of the folded cloth was like a pocket. Inside they put the Urim V'Tumim. The Urim V'Tumim

The multicolored cloth used to make the Kohen Gadol's Bigdei Kehunah was made by weaving together fibers made of five different colored threads. The threads were white twisted flax combined with blue, purple, and red colored wool as well as a gold thread.

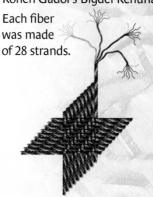

The fibers were made in a very special way. Six threads of purple wool were twisted together to make a purple thread. The same was done with six threads each of twisted flax and the blue and red colored wool. A gold thread was twisted together with each different colored thick thread.

There were now four threads of different colors — white flax, red, purple, and blue wool, each with gold. They were twisted together to make multicolored fibers. These fibers were then woven to make the cloth for the Kohen Gadol's Bigdei Kehunah.

Each fiber was made of 28 strands.

had the secret holy Name of Hashem written on it.

The Choshen, with its Urim V'Tumim, could answer questions put to it by the Kohen Gadol or the king. The Name of Hashem inside gave the Choshen the power to do that.

12 Stones

Twelve gold boxes were attached to the front of the Choshen. Into these were placed 12 precious stones. Each had one of the names of the shevatim carved on it.

Reuven's stone also had the names of Avraham, Yitzchak, and Yaakov carved on it. And carved into Binyamin's stone were the words "Shivtei Yeshurun" — the Tribes of Yeshurun, another name for the Jewish nation. These extra words were necessary so that the Choshen would have all the letters of the Hebrew alphabet on it.

Colors/Stones/Names

Here is a chart of the name and color of each shevet's stone:

SHEVET	STONE	COLOR
רְאוּבֵן, REUVEN	אֹדֶם, ODEM	RED
שִׁמְעוֹן, SHIMON	פִּטְדָה, PIT'DAH	GREEN
לֵוִי, LEVI	בָּרֶקֶת, BAREKES	1/3 WHITE, 1/3 BLACK, 1/3 RED
יְהוּדָה, YEHUDAH	נֹפֶךְ, NOFECH	SKY BLUE
יִשָּׂשכָר, YISSACHAR	סַפִּיר, SAPIR	MIDNIGHT BLUE
זְבוּלֻן, ZEVULUN	יַהֲלֹם, YAHALOM	WHITE
דָן, DAN	לֶשֶׁם, LESHEM	MIDNIGHT BLUE
נַפְתָּלִי, NAFTALI	שְׁבוֹ, SHEVO	BLACK AND WHITE MIXED
גָּד, GAD	אַחְלָמָה, ACHLAMAH	BLUSH
אָשֵׁר, ASHER	תַּרְשִׁישׁ, TARSHISH	DIAMOND
יוֹסֵף, YOSEF	שֹׁהַם, SHOHAM	DEEP BLACK
בִּנְיָמִין, BINYAMIN	יָשְׁפֵה, YASHFEH	THE COLORS OF ALL THE OTHER STONES

The Shamir Worm

The names on the Shoham and Choshen stones had to be engraved into the stones. But the stones had to be kept whole. If they used a sharp metal to scratch the names into the stone, small pieces of stone would be chipped away, so the stones wouldn't be whole! What did they do?

FASCINATING FACTS

The word שֹׁהַם, "shoham," has three Hebrew letters — shin, hei, and mem. These are the same letters as in the name "Moshe" and in the word "Hashem." The names of the twelve shevatim were inscribed on the stones. The Shoham stones symbolized the close relationship between Hashem, Moshe, and the Jewish people.

QUESTIONS, ANYONE?

How did the Urim V'Tumim answer questions?

Sometimes the king or the nation had an important question they needed Hashem to answer. Questions like: Should we go to war or not? How do we divide Eretz Yisrael among the shevatim?

They would ask the Kohen Gadol the question. He would look down at the Choshen, and certain letters would light up. Hashem would let the Kohen Gadol know how to read the order of the letters that he saw. The Kohen Gadol would tell everyone what Hashem answered.

They used a shamir. This was a worm that Hashem created at twilight of the first Erev Shabbos of Creation. It had amazing powers — and it could make cracks in the stone in the shape of the letters.

The names of each shevet were written on the stone in ink. Then they put the shamir on the stone, and it cracked the stone in the shape of the letters, without chipping anything away.

Golden Cords

Golden cords attached the Choshen to the Ephod straps. A gold ring was sewn onto the top two corners of the Choshen. Golden cord was passed through the rings. The other ends of the cords were attached to gold settings at the ends of the Ephod's shoulder straps.

More Rings

Gold rings were attached to each of the two bottom corners of the back side of the Choshen, so that they were against the Ephod. In order to keep the Choshen firmly in place, a string of blue wool passed through the rings of the Choshen.

The blue string then went around the back of the Kohen, where they passed through the rings at the bottom of the shoulder straps of the Ephod, and the string was tied.

Me'il / Robe
A Long Blue Robe

The Kohen Gadol wore the Me'il — a blue robe that reached the floor and had long sleeves. The Me'il was made entirely of techeiles (specially-dyed wool). The part of the Me'il that he wore on his body was woven as one piece, not like a regular robe, which has different pieces sewn together. Each sleeve was woven as one separate piece. The two sleeves were sewn onto the Me'il.

The neck hole of the Me'il was woven to be twice as thick as the rest of the Me'il. This kept it from tearing.

Bells and Pomegranates

When the Kohen Gadol walked you could hear him coming, because small gold bells were attached all around the bottom of the Me'il. As he walked, the bells moved and rang.

Between the bells hung tear-shaped balls of cloth. These were called "pomegranates" because when pomegranates first begin to grow, they are shaped like tears.

The balls of cloth were hollow and were woven from blue, purple, and red wool.

Tzitz / Headplate

A Plate of Gold

Across his forehead, the Kohen Gadol wore a plate of gold, the height of two thumb-widths. It was called the Tzitz and it stretched from ear to ear.

The words "Kodesh LaHashem," Holy to Hashem, were written on the Tzitz. The Name of Hashem appeared on the first line and under it, on the second line, was the word "kodesh" and the letter "lamed." Some opinions say the words were written on one line.

Blue Ribbons

On the top and sides of the Tzitz were slots through which they inserted wide blue ribbons. The Kohen Gadol took the side ribbons and wrapped them around the sides of his head. The top ribbons went over the two sides of his head covering.

The ribbons were tied together behind his head, at his neck.

THE BIGDEI KEHUNAH OF THE KOHEN HEDYOT

There were four items that all Kohanim wore, including the Kohen Gadol.

Kutones / Shirt
Pure White

Every Kohen wore a long shirt that covered his entire body. It was made of pure white linen. The linen was woven with a pattern of small boxes all over.

Like the Me'il, the Kutones was woven in three separate pieces — two sleeves, and the part that covered the body. Each piece was woven as one whole piece. Then the sleeves were sewn onto the large shirt.

The sleeves were as wide as the Kohen's arm and reached till his palm. The shirt went from his shoulders to the ground, without dragging on the floor. Some Kohanim were short and others tall, some had long arms and others short. Each Kutones was made to fit the Kohen!

Migbaas, Mitznefes / Hat

A Cone-Shaped Hat

The Migbaas was a hat that was worn like a turban. The Kohen was given a long, narrow piece of linen cloth that he wrapped around his head to look like a high cone. The Kohen Gadol's hat was the same, and was called the Mitznefes.

Avnet / Belt

A Long Belt

The Avnet was a belt made of multicolored fabric. It was 32 amos long (64 feet!). It was not a simple piece of fabric. It was woven like a hollow tube and then flattened to look like a sash.

Because it was so long, the Kohen would wind the Avnet many times around and around and around his body. By the time he finished, the belt was a wide band of color on his pure white Kutones.

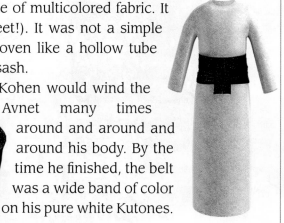

Michnasayim / Short Pants

These were made of linen. When the Kohen put them on he tightened their drawstrings right above his navel. The pants reached his knees.

GETTING DRESSED

The Kohanim got dressed in a certain specific order. Let's first look at how the Kohen Gadol would dress.

After putting on his Michnasayim (short pants), the Kohen Gadol put on his Kutones (shirt), then the Avnet (belt).

Then came the Me'il (blue robe). Then he tied the Ephod (apron) and the Choshen to it. Now he wrapped the Mitznefes (hat) around

FASCINATING FACTS

There used to be a custom that on the day of his wedding a bridegroom wore a crown on his head. But after the Beis HaMikdash was destroyed and the Kohen Gadol no longer crowned his head with a Mitznefes, bridegrooms stopped wearing crowns.

When the Kohen Gadol entered the Kodesh HaKodashim on Yom Kippur, he wore only four pieces of the Bigdei Kehunah, just like the other Kohanim: the Kutones, Michnasayim, Mitznefes, and Avnet. But unlike the rest of the year, the belt he wore when entering the Kodesh was made of white linen. The Kohen Gadol dressed in white as a symbol of purity and holiness.

his head. He then placed the Tzitz (headplate) on his forehead and tied its ribbons over his hat and around his head.

This is what it looked like when he was finished getting dressed:

Royalty

Imagine seeing Aharon after he put on his Bigdei Kehunah. With the jewels of the Choshen and the Ephod sparkling in the sun, he looked like a king. And with his glowing face framed by his beard and the Tzitz on his forehead, he looked like a holy angel.

The Kohen Hedyot

The Kohen Hedyot would first put on Michnasayim (short pants), then the Kutones (shirt); next he would wrap the Avnet (belt) around his waist.

Finally he put on the Migbaas (hat). Though his hat had a different name from the Mitznefes (hat) of the Kohen Gadol, they were the same: It was a long piece of linen wrapped around his head like a turban.

Here is what a Kohen Hedyot looked like:

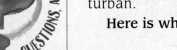

Where is the description of the shoes the Kohen wore in the Mishkan?

Don't look too hard! The Kohanim didn't wear any shoes in the Mishkan. They did all the services barefoot!

GETTING READY!

Hashem had taught the Jews how to build the Mishkan and make the clothes for the Kohanim. He had chosen Aharon and his sons and their descendants to be the Kohanim. They would serve in the Mishkan and eventually in the Beis HaMikdash.

Now Hashem told Moshe how to prepare Aharon and his sons to do their awesome job of serving in the Mishkan. They could not just walk in on the first day and begin to serve. Aharon and his sons had to go through an entire week, seven days of training, before they would be able to begin their work as Kohanim. During those seven days, while Moshe himself served as Kohen Gadol, Aharon and his sons would learn what to do and become pure, holy, and special. Through what they did during those seven days they would become the only Jewish family who were permitted to work in the Mishkan.

Actions

Every day, for seven days, Aharon and his sons did the following:

▸ First, they purified themselves in a mikvah before entering the Mishkan.

▸ Moshe dressed Aharon in his Bigdei Kehunah. He poured a small amount of oil on Aharon's head. The oil was called the Shemen HaMishchah.

▸ Moshe then dressed Aharon's children. He put the Avnet on each one of them, and on Aharon as well.

▸ Moshe then offered the korbanos and sprinkled and smeared blood and oil on Aharon and his children.

▸ They spent the day in the Mishkan. Moshe also spent the day in the Mishkan, offering their korbanos.

Bread, Bulls, and Rams

On each of the seven days a bull and two rams were brought to the Mishkan. The bull would become a Korban Chatas (sin offering). It would bring forgiveness for the sin of the Eigel HaZahav and it would make the Copper Mizbei'ach holy.

One ram would become a Korban Olah (burnt offering). This animal would be totally burnt on the Mizbei'ach.

The other ram would become a Korban Shelamim (peace offering).

In addition to the korbanos, three types of matzos — matzah bread, matzah loaves, and matzah wafers — were prepared. There were ten of each type, making a total of 30 matzos.

Matzah x 3

Matzah bread was made by mixing flour with water. Boiling water was then poured on the dough to cook it, it was baked in an oven, and finally fried in oil.

Matzah loaves were made by mixing flour and water, adding oil, and then baking it.

Matzah wafers were made by mixing flour and water and baking them. After baking, they were smeared with oil.

Although they are not chametz, we do not use such matzos on Pesach.

Kohen for a Week

During the seven days of preparation, Moshe acted as the Kohen, performing the Mishkan services. He was the one who sprinkled blood and put the animal parts on the Mizbei'ach. After that week was over, only Kohanim would serve in the Mishkan.

WHO'S WHO IN THE TORAH

Aharon had four sons:
Nadav, Avihu, Elazar, and Issamar

Nadav and Avihu would die on the day the regular services began in the Mishkan. (We will read about that in Parashas Shemini.)

Later, when his father Aharon died, Elazar was appointed to be the new Kohen Gadol. His son was Pinchas, who we will read about in Parashas Pinchas.

The Bull

After shechitah, the blood of the bull was put on the horns of the Copper Mizbei'ach. The fat that covered its insides, the muscle that is right under the lungs (diaphragm), part of the liver, its kidneys and their fat were burned on the Mizbei'ach.

The rest of the animal was burned outside the place where the Jewish people camped.

Ram #1

After shechitah, the blood of the first ram was sprinkled on the Mizbei'ach. All the parts of the animal were burned on the Copper Mizbei'ach.

Ram #2

After shechitah, unlike the other korbanos, the blood of the second ram wasn't sprinkled on the Mizbei'ach right away. First some blood was put on Aharon and his sons.

If you touch the middle of your ear you will feel something hard sticking out from the rest of the ear. It feels like a soft bone. It was on this part of the right ear that Moshe smeared the ram's blood on Aharon and his sons.

Then he put some on the thumb of their right hand and finally on the big toe of their right foot.

Blood and Oil

Some of the second ram's blood was sprinkled on the Mizbei'ach. Moshe then took some of the blood that was on the Mizbei'ach and some of the special anointing oil, Shemen HaMishchah, and sprinkled them on Aharon and his sons and on their special clothing. This made Aharon, his sons, and their Bigdei Kehunah holy to Hashem, so that they could do the Mishkan service.

All Around, Up and Down

Moshe took the ram's fat and put it on Aharon's outstretched hands. On top of that he put all the parts of the ram that would be burned on the Mizbei'ach.

Remember the three types of matzos that were baked? Now Moshe took one of each type and put it on top of the pile on Aharon's hands.

TORAH IN OUR LIVES

We all know that if a pilot doesn't follow the instructions of the air traffic controller, the passengers will be in danger.

A Kohen is like a pilot. If he doesn't carefully follow Hashem's instructions on what to do in the Mishkan, and perform the service properly… the Jews will not receive all of Hashem's blessings.

That is why Hashem had Moshe put the ram's blood on the ears of the Kohanim. It was to warn them to listen carefully to Hashem's instructions.

In addition, blood was put on the thumbs of their right hand and foot to teach them to use their hands and feet to do the Mishkan services correctly.

This is a message to us as well. As we go through life, we have to listen carefully to the instructions of Hashem's Torah. We must be sure to do the mitzvos correctly, even if we do not understand why, so we get safely to where Hashem wants us to go.

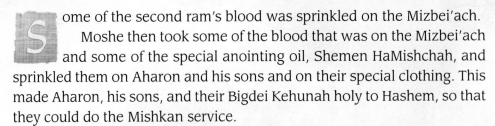

Moshe put his hands under Aharon's. Together they moved their hands all around — east, west, north, and south (some say they wave it only back and forth), and then up and down. This is called the service of Tenufah (waving). Then the Tenufah was done with Aharon's sons. Finally, Moshe took everything and put it all on the Mizbei'ach to be burned.

Mealtime

They then did Tenufah with the chest of the second ram, and it then belonged to Moshe, for him to eat.

The rest of the meat of the second ram was given to Aharon and his sons. They cooked and ate it in the Chatzer (Courtyard of the Mishkan), which was enclosed by curtains.

With their meal they ate the 27 matzos that were still left.

This procedure was repeated every day for seven days. Then Aharon and his sons were ready to serve as Kohanim.

Something's Missing

Not only the Kohanim had to be prepared. The Copper Mizbei'ach also had to become holy. So during the very same seven days that Aharon and his sons were preparing themselves, Moshe was preparing the Copper Mizbei'ach, on which he brought the Korban Chatas. It became holy when Moshe anointed it with the special anointing oil, the Shemen HaMishchah.

SOME OF THE MISHKAN SERVICES

Korban Tamid — The Daily Offering

Every Day

Hashem said that every morning and late afternoon, a lamb should be brought as a korban. Its blood should be put on the Copper Mizbei'ach and the lamb's body burned there. This was called the Korban Tamid.

Along with the lamb, the Kohen brought flour and oil that were mixed together and burned on the Mizbei'ach. He also poured wine on the Mizbei'ach. The wine was poured into a small hole on top of the Mizbei'ach.

QUESTIONS, ANYONE?

Why did they do Tenufah, waving the meat to the sides and up and down?

1. Tornadoes and hurricanes are examples of harmful and dangerous winds. They blow from all sides: north, west, south and east. Doing the Tenufah service keeps these kinds of dangerous winds away from us.

   Moving the meat up and down protects the crops from harmful dew.

2. This also shows that Hashem sees everything that is going on in the world, in all four directions and up and down. Hashem watches over every single person. There is nowhere in the world that Hashem does not see and where a person could hide from Him!

Amounts

The amounts of flour, oil, and wine brought with each lamb were:

Flour	1/10 of an eifah	About 14 cups
Oil	¼ of a hin	About 35 ounces
Wine	¼ of a hin	About 35 ounces

Mizbach HaZahav — The Golden Altar

Ketores (Incense)

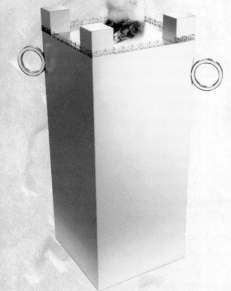

The Golden Mizbei'ach stood in the Mishkan's front section, together with the Menorah and Shulchan. Every day, once in the morning and once in the afternoon, a special incense made for the Mishkan was burned on this Mizbei'ach. This is why it's also called the Mizbach HaKetores. On Yom Kippur, blood of some of the Yom Kippur korbanos was sprinkled on this Mizbei'ach.

Smoke and Fire

For the daily Ketores service, the Kohen would go to the copper Mizbei'ach that stood in the Chatzer. He would go up the ramp to the top, and take a shovelful of glowing hot coals from the burning fires.

He then entered the Mishkan building and put the coals on the Golden Mizbei'ach. After that, about ten ounces of specially prepared Ketores was put on the coals. Smoke would rise in a straight column, hit the ceiling, and fill the room with smoke.

All Alone

When the Kohen was burning the daily Ketores, no one else was allowed in the Mishkan building or even in the area between the entrance of the Mishkan and the Copper Mizbei'ach.

Gold

The Golden Mizbei'ach was made of shittim wood covered with gold on all its sides, even the top. It was shaped like a tall square box. It was one amah square and two amos high (approximately two feet square and four feet high). At each top corner were four small boxes sticking up. They were called the "horns" of the Mizbei'ach.

The letters of the word Ketores (קְטֹרֶת) are the initials of:

ק·kedushah — holiness
ט·taharah —purity
ר·rachamim —mercy
ת·tikvah —hope

The smell of the burning Ketores was so powerful that its sweet scent could be smelled in the air all the way from Yerushalayim to Yericho — fifteen miles away!

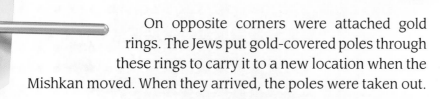

On opposite corners were attached gold rings. The Jews put gold-covered poles through these rings to carry it to a new location when the Mishkan moved. When they arrived, the poles were taken out.

In the Middle

The Golden Mizbei'ach was placed in middle of the front section of the Mishkan building. This area was known as the Kodesh. Past this Mizbei'ach on the left side stood the Menorah, and on the right was the Shulchan.

Gold Crown

At the top of the Mizbei'ach was a gold decoration that looked like a gold crown. This crown was a symbol of the special status of Kohanim, a reminder that only they could perform the holy services in the Mishkan and Beis HaMikdash.

Lottery

All Kohanim wanted a chance to perform the service of burning the Ketores. The reward for doing this special mitzvah was a blessing for wealth. With so many people wanting to do this service, how did they decide who should do it?

There was a lottery. The Kohanim would stand in a circle and stick

TORAH IN OUR LIVES

Is there any connection between burning Ketores on the Golden Mizbei'ach and our lives today? The answer is … Yes!

As a matter of fact, this mitzvah can, in a way, be performed today. How? By being a sandek at a bris. A sandek is the man who holds the baby on his lap while the mohel is doing the bris.

Our Sages teach us that the sandek is like a Kohen who burns the Ketores on the Golden Mizbei'ach in the Beis HaMikdash.

When you grow up and have the chance to become a sandek, don't think twice. Grab the opportunity!

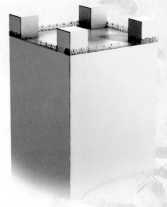

out a finger. A number was picked randomly. The Kohen in charge would count the fingers around the circle until he got to the number picked. That Kohen got to do the service.

Any Kohen who had done the service once, couldn't be in the lottery ever again. It was a once-in-a-lifetime opportunity.

פָּרָשַׁת
כִּי תִשָּׂא
•
Parashas
Ki Sisa

Ki Sisa · כִּי תִשָּׂא

Parashah Pointers

▸ Hashem tells Moshe that when he counts the Jewish men from the age of twenty and up, he should collect a silver half-shekel from each man. By counting the half-shekels, Moshe will know how many Jewish men there are.

▸ Hashem commands Moshe to make a Kiyor. The Kiyor was like a large copper pot of water. Before starting their day's Mishkan service, the Kohanim had to wash their hands and feet from water that came out from spouts.

▸ Hashem gives Moshe the recipe to make a special oil called Shemen HaMishchah. A bit of this sweet-smelling oil was to be smeared on the Mishkan and all the items used there to make them holy. The oil was also put on the heads of Aharon and his sons to make them holy.

▸ Hashem tells the Jews how to make the Ketores, a wonderful-smelling incense that was burned on the Golden Mizbei'ach every day, and in the Kodash HaKodashim on Yom Kippur.

▸ Hashem tells the Jews to keep Shabbos.

▸ The Jews make the Eigel HaZahav, the Golden Calf.

▸ Moshe is given the Luchos, the Tablets on which the Aseres HaDibros (Ten Commandments) are written.

▸ When Moshe sees the Jews dancing around the Eigel HaZahav, he breaks the Luchos and destroys the Eigel.

▸ Shevet Levi puts to death people who worshiped the Eigel.

▸ Moshe goes back up Har Sinai for 40 days and prays that Hashem should forgive the Jews.

▸ Hashem forgives the Jews and teaches Moshe the best way to pray.

▸ Hashem tells Moshe to carve out two new Tablets.

▸ When Moshe comes down from Har Sinai his face is shining.

Let's Count

Hashem told Moshe that when he counts the Jewish men, age twenty to sixty, this is how he should do it. Each man should give a silver half-shekel. When the half-shekels are counted, they will know how many Jewish men there are.

Then Hashem commanded Moshe to collect half-shekels from all men who were age twenty to sixty.

These coins were counted, and they were then melted down and made into silver blocks called Adanim. The beams of the Mishkan rested in these blocks.

Three Kinds of Gifts

The Jews in the desert gave three kinds of donations:

1. The half-shekel given to count the men between 20 and 60.

2. Another half-shekel from each man. This half-shekel would be given every year. The money was used to buy the korbanos that were brought in the Mishkan and the Beis HaMikdash for the entire nation. Hashem wanted everyone to have a share in the korbanos.

3. Gold, silver, copper, and other materials that were used to make the Mishkan and the clothing of the Kohanim. Some people gave more and some gave less. It was up to each Jew to decide what and how much to give.

Remembering a Mitzvah

On the Shabbos before Rosh Chodesh Adar — or, if Rosh Chodesh is on Shabbos, on Rosh Chodesh itself — we read Parashas Shekalim. Besides the regular Parashas HaShavuah, on that Shabbos we also read the first six pesukim of this parashah, which talk about the mitzvah of Machatzis HaShekel. Why do we do this?

The Machatzis HaShekel, the silver half-shekel that was used for communal korbanos brought in the Beis HaMikdash, was collected during the month of Adar. On the first of Nissan they would start using the "new" money that had just been collected.

The Beis HaMikdash is destroyed. We can't do this mitzvah anymore. But we want to remember how things were when we had the Beis HaMikdash. So instead of doing the mitzvah, we read about it in the Torah, right before the beginning of Adar, the month when the coins used to be collected.

QUESTIONS, ANYONE?

Hashem asked for a half-shekel each, not less, not more. But if someone is rich and wants to give more, why can't he?

1. The half-shekel was given to make up for the sin of the Eigel HaZahav. The sin began when half a day had passed and Moshe did not come down from Sinai as the Jews had expected (see page 160). They panicked and made the idol. Hashem commanded them to give a half-shekel for the mistake they made at midday.

2. A half-shekel is equal to 10 geirah (a small coin used in those days – the way a dime is equal to ten pennies). This half-shekel was a symbol that when they sinned with the Eigel HaZahav, the Jews disobeyed what was written in the Ten Commandments.

3. No matter how rich a Jew is, he should never feel that he is whole just by himself. He's only a half. He is not a complete person unless he is connected with his fellow Jew. To be the best Jew he can be, he needs other Jews.

FASCINATING FACTS

These laws about donating silver were given to the Jews on Yom Kippur — the day Moshe came down from Sinai with the second set of Luchos.

TORAH IN OUR LIVES

We wash our hands from a cup when we wake up in the morning, the way the Kohanim did before doing their service in the Mishkan.

Similarly, before Kohanim go to say Bircas Kohanim, when they bless the Jews, they also wash their hands.

There is also a custom to give three half-dollar coins to tzedakah (charity) on Taanis Esther, to remember the three kinds of donations that the Jews gave in the desert.

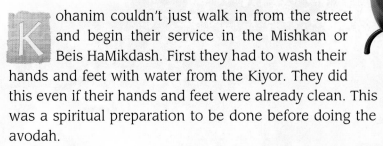

Wash Up

Kohanim couldn't just walk in from the street and begin their service in the Mishkan or Beis HaMikdash. First they had to wash their hands and feet with water from the Kiyor. They did this even if their hands and feet were already clean. This was a spiritual preparation to be done before doing the avodah.

The Kiyor was like a very large copper pot filled with water. It rested on a copper stand. The water flowed out of spouts.

When a Kohen entered the Mishkan, he would first head to the ramp of the Copper Mizbei'ach, which stood in the Chatzer. The Kiyor was on the side of the ramp opposite the entrance of the Mishkan.

He would bend down, then put his right hand on his right foot and his left hand on his left foot. Then he would let the water from the Kiyor pour over them.

Shemen HaMishchah

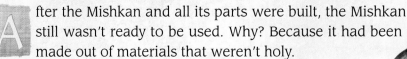

After the Mishkan and all its parts were built, the Mishkan still wasn't ready to be used. Why? Because it had been made out of materials that weren't holy.

How could the Mishkan and everything in it be made holy and ready to serve Hashem?

Hashem told Moshe to make a special, sweet-smelling oil, Shemen HaMishchah, and to smear some of it on every part of the Mishkan and all its items. That was how everything in the Mishkan would become holy.

Putting Oil on the Leaders

The oil had another use as well. It was put on the heads of:

▸ Aharon and his sons

▸ A new Kohen Gadol

▸ King Shaul

▸ King David

▸ Any king from the House of David, but only if there was an argument about whether he should become king

Shemen HaMishchah Don'ts

There were special rules about the Shemen HaMishchah.

No one is allowed to make Shemen HaMishchah the same way Moshe made it.

No one was allowed to smear Moshe's Shemen HaMishchah on himself or anyone else. It could be put only on the Mishkan, its utensils, the Kohen Gadol, and kings.

Ketores - The Holy Incense

The Torah gives the recipe to make the Ketores. This specially made incense was burned on the Golden Mizbei'ach every day. On Yom Kippur, the holiest day of the year, it was burned in the Kodash HaKodashim. It contained 11 spices that were ground into a powder. When the powder was burned it gave off a beautiful smell. (For more on the Ketores, see Parashas Tetzaveh, page 152.)

Ketores Don'ts

Since the Ketores had such a wonderful smell, someone might want to copy it and make some for personal use. The Torah warns that this is not allowed. However, a person may make it and sell it for use in the Beis HaMikdash.

The Supervisor

Hashem told Moshe to appoint Betzalel to be in charge of the building of the Mishkan. His assistant would be Ohaliav. Besides supervising, they also helped build the Mishkan. (To read more about them, see Parashas Vayakhel, page 180.)

Shabbos

The Torah now tells us to keep Shabbos. Shabbos will forever be a symbol of the unbreakable agreement between the Jews and Hashem. By keeping Shabbos, we declare that Hashem created the world in six days and rested on the seventh day.

FASCINATING FACTS

Right before we begin the Shemoneh Esrei of Friday night, most shuls say two pesukim that begin with the words "V'shamru Bnei Yisrael…", the Jewish people kept the Shabbos as our eternal agreement with Hashem. These two pesukim are in this parashah.

Though it was a terrible thing, something very good also happened because of the sin of the Eigel.

Can you think of anything worse? The Jews were on such a high and holy level that Hashem actually spoke to them at Sinai. Yet only forty days after hearing Hashem Himself tell them not to have any other gods, and not to make statues, they committed the terrible sin of the Eigel HaZahav.

Yet after the Jews did teshuvah, Hashem forgave them! This teaches us that no matter what bad things we do, Hashem loves us. He is like parents who love their children even if they do bad things.

We should remember this when we feel we did something Hashem will not forgive us for. That's not true! No matter what we did in the past, no matter how bad it was, Hashem still loves us and is waiting for us to do teshuvah and come back to Him. And when we do teshuvah, He accepts us with open hands.

Six pesukim in our parashah teach us many things about Shabbos. Here are some of them:

▸ Even though the Mishkan is very important, we are not permitted to build it on Shabbos.

▸ We should look forward to Shabbos. We should be happy when Shabbos begins.

▸ We may — actually, we must — break the rules of Shabbos to save a person's life. When a life is in danger, it is called "pikuach nefesh."

▸ On Shabbos we are blessed with an extra soul that stays with us until Shabbos is over.

▸ If the Jewish people will keep two Shabbosos, one after the other, Mashiach will come.

The Sin of the Eigel HaZahav

The sin of the Eigel HaZahav, the Golden Calf, was a terrible tragedy. If it hadn't happened, today's world would be so different.

The Jews would have been immortal forever!

We would all be living in Eretz Yisrael with the Beis HaMikdash instead of being spread out all over the world.

We lost that wonderful world because of the sin. And even more, every time Hashem punishes the Jewish nation for doing something wrong, a little extra bit of punishment is added for the sin of the Eigel.

The story begins with a small mistake that turned into a huge sin.

Eirev Rav

Before we continue the story and tell what happened next, we need to know about the Eirev Rav.

Who were they?

When the Jews left Egypt, many Egyptians and other non-Jews who saw the miracles realized that Hashem was the one and only true G-d. They wanted to join the Jews and leave Egypt with them.

Without asking Hashem what to do, Moshe converted them.

The Eirev Rav were the main troublemakers in the story of the Eigel HaZahav. They were the ones who began bowing and worshiping it. As a result, other Jews joined them. Although many Jews did not join, Shevet Levi was the only shevet where not one member of the shevet joined in worshiping the Eigel!

Moshe Is Late

I t was the 16th day of Tammuz and the Jews were nervous. Forty days before, Moshe had left them to go up to Har Sinai to get the Torah. He had told them he would be back in forty days. It was already past midday. Where was he?

Panic!

N ow the Satan saw his chance! He would cause panic among the Jews. Then it would be easy to get them to sin.

The Satan put an image in the sky. It looked like Moshe lying dead. Looking up, the Jews saw it. That terrified them.

They pointed to the image and said, "It's Moshe Rabbeinu! Look what happened to him! He is not coming back!"

The Jews panicked. What would they do? Here they were, stranded in the middle of the desert! Who would take care of them and their families now that Moshe was gone?

Murder!

A haron and his nephew, Chur, who was Miriam's son, had been put in charge while Moshe was gone. The Jews came running to Chur.

"We need to replace Moshe!" they shouted. "Make us a god that we can worship!"

"What is with you?!" Chur demanded. "Where is your faith? Don't you remember all the miracles Hashem has done for us? Would He let something happen to Moshe? Impossible! What you saw was the Satan's doing!"

The Jews didn't like his answer. The mob killed him.

Give Me Your Gold

N ext, they turned to Aharon, and demanded that he make an idol. They threatened to do to Aharon what they did to Chur. Aharon said to himself, *If I say no, they will kill me just like they killed Chur. If they do that, Hashem will send them into exile, because they would have killed both a prophet and a Kohen. So, to save the Jewish nation from destruction, I will agree. But I will do everything as slowly as I can, to give Moshe time to come back before the Jews have time to do anything bad.*

So Aharon told the Jews to bring him the gold jewelry of their wives and children. He knew that would take time. It wouldn't be easy for the men

FASCINATING FACTS

The Jews had made a mistake. When Moshe said he would be back in 40 days, he meant 40 full days. That did not include the day he went up Har Sinai. He wasn't late — the Jews had misunderstood him.

QUESTIONS, ANYONE?

What was the women's reward for not giving their jewelry to create the Eigel?

Rosh Chodesh. The women didn't sin, so Rosh Chodesh, the beginning of the new month, became a partial holiday for them. On Rosh Chodesh women try to avoid doing difficult jobs, like washing clothes and sewing.

How did an Eigel come out?
There are a few answers:

1. There were wizards among the Eirev Rav, the Egyptians who joined the Jews when they left Egypt. Using the power of evil magic that the Satan gave them, they caused the calf to jump out of the fire complete and ready-made.

2. After Pharaoh made the law that the Jews would not be given straw to make bricks (see page 21), he added that if a person didn't make enough bricks, their children would be used as bricks, cementing them into the walls of the buildings!

Moshe asked Hashem how He could let such a thing happen. Hashem answered, "If these children had lived, they would have been wicked. If you'd like, take out one of the babies and you will see that I was right."

Moshe chose a baby named Michah.

Michah is the reason the Golden Calf jumped out of the fire.

Michah was there when Moshe brought Yosef's casket up out of the deep waters of the Nile by throwing a metal plate (some opinions say it was a piece of pottery) into the Nile. On that plate were the words "alei shor — rise up, ox." An ox was the symbol of Yosef. Yosef's bones came up when the plate went into the water.

When Moshe left with Yosef's bones, Michah took the metal plate and kept it.

Now, when he saw Aharon throw the gold into the fire, Michah threw in the metal plate. And that caused a calf — which is a young ox — to rise out of the fire.

to convince their wives and children to give up their jewelry to make the Eigel HaZahav.

We Refuse!

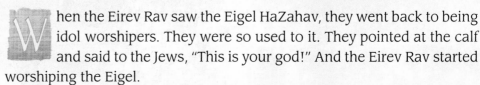

he men went home and told their wives what they were planning to do, and they asked for their gold jewelry. The righteous Jewish women told the men, "We refuse! We won't give you anything! What are you doing? It's wrong! We don't want to be part of such a sin!"

The men didn't want to waste time arguing with their wives, so they ran back to Aharon and gave him their own gold jewelry.

Moshe still hadn't appeared.

Ready-Made!

haron took the gold and threw it into a fire, hoping it would take a long time to make it into an idol. First the gold had to melt. Then it had to cool down. Then he would start making the statue, and before he would finish, Moshe would be back.

But that didn't happen.

After Aharon threw the gold into the fire, out jumped a ready-made, instant Golden Calf!

Delay, Delay

hen the Eirev Rav saw the Eigel HaZahav, they went back to being idol worshipers. They were so used to it. They pointed at the calf and said to the Jews, "This is your god!" And the Eirev Rav started worshiping the Eigel.

The Jews didn't believe such nonsense. But they didn't stop the Eirev Rav. There were even some Jews who began to think ... maybe they are right?

Aharon saw that things were getting worse and worse. He had to find a way to stop them. He had to delay them until Moshe came down.

"I will build an altar for it," he announced. Because Aharon built it himself, he took a long time building it.

The altar was finished but ... Moshe still didn't appear.

Tomorrow

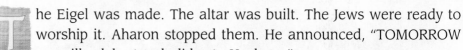

he Eigel was made. The altar was built. The Jews were ready to worship it. Aharon stopped them. He announced, "TOMORROW we will celebrate a holiday to Hashem."

Everyone went home to get ready. They would worship the calf tomorrow.

The day before the Torah was given, the Jews declared, "Naaseh v'nishma — whatever Hashem wants we will do and we will listen." Agreeing to do what Hashem wanted without even knowing what He wanted them to do was an enormous good deed. Hashem rewarded them with the sudden appearance of 600,000 angels, who gave each Jew two crowns. One was a reward for saying "Naaseh — we will do," and another was a reward for saying "v'nishma — and we will listen."

Because of the sin of the Eigel HaZahav, now 1,200,000 destructive angels were sent to take the two crowns back to heaven.

The entire time Moshe was in heaven he didn't eat, drink, or sleep.

TORAH IN OUR LIVES

If Hashem gifted Moshe to remember the whole Torah after 40 days of learning, why didn't He just give Moshe the gift on the very first day? The answer is that Moshe's gift was a reward for 39 days of trying hard to master the Torah.

When it comes to Torah, the main thing is to try hard. The effort we put into our learning is what is important. If Hashem gave you a good head to learn easily — keep trying harder, learn more and more! And if you have different talents, but learning is hard for you, remember that Hashem wants and loves your effort — and He will reward you for trying!

Morning

On the morning after the Eigel was made, the seventeenth of Tammuz, the Jews had no problem getting up early. The Satan made sure they didn't sleep late so they could sin as soon as possible.

The Jews sacrificed animals, worshiped the Eigel and made a grand party. The sin that Aharon tried so hard to prevent, the sin of the Eigel HaZahav — had happened. Disaster and catastrophe!

When Hashem saw what the Jews were doing, He grew very angry.

Meanwhile ... Up in Heaven

Meanwhile, for the past forty days and nights, Moshe had been awake learning with Hashem in heaven. As hard as he tried, Moshe kept forgetting the Torah Hashem taught him. Finally, on the last day, Hashem gave him a gift — he would remember what he learned. Now Moshe knew and remembered the entire Torah.

Because Moshe was in heaven, he didn't know what was going on down below. But then Hashem told him, "Go down because your nation, which you took out of Egypt, has become evil."

"Leave Me Alone"

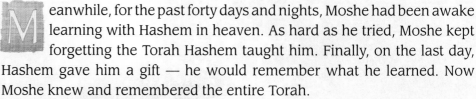

Moshe asked Hashem, "Why do You call them my nation? They are Your nation."

Hashem answered, "It was the Eirev Rav, whom you allowed to join the Jews, who sinned and who caused the Jews to sin."

Hashem told Moshe what had happened while he was away.

"They made a Golden Calf and bowed down to it," He said. "They shouted, 'Jews, this is your god, who took you out of Egypt!' I see these people are stubborn and won't listen to criticism. Leave Me alone, and in My anger I will destroy them. I will create a new Jewish nation from you and your children."

Moshe heard Hashem's words, "leave Me alone," and he realized that Hashem was giving him a hint. It was as if Hashem was saying to him: "It's up to you. If you leave Me alone I will destroy them — and if you **don't leave Me alone** and you pray for them, I will forgive them."

Moshe immediately began to pray and defend the Jews as hard as he could.

Moshe the Defender

With great courage, like a roaring lion, Moshe defended the Jews. "Why are You getting angry at Your people, whom You took out of Egypt?" he said. "What did You expect? Out of all the places in the world to exile them, You put them in Egypt, one of the worst idol-worshiping nations on earth! Is it their fault that they worshiped the Eigel HaZahav? They learned idol worship from being in Egypt — where You put them!"

What Will the Egyptians Say?

Moshe continued to speak. "The Egyptians will hear that You destroyed the Jews. You know what they will say? That You didn't take them out to save them, but to destroy them. They will say that You have power only to destroy."

Remember!

Moshe continued, "Don't be angry. Have mercy on Your nation. Forgive them because of the outstanding good deeds that Avraham, Yitzchak, and Yaakov did for You.

"If You punish them for going against the Aseres HaDibros, remember Avraham, who hasn't yet been rewarded for the ten difficult tests he passed. Let his ten tests cancel the Jews' punishment for disobeying the Aseres HaDibros — and don't punish them.

"Are You going to destroy them through fire? Remember Avraham, who was thrown into the fire because he refused to say that there were other gods besides You — and forgive them.

"If you are going to destroy them by sword, remember Yitzchak, who was ready to die by the sword at Akeidas Yitzchak — and forgive them.

"If You are going to destroy them with exile, remember the good deeds of Yaakov, who lived for many years in exile with Lavan and in Egypt — and FORGIVE THEM!"

Success!

Moshe's words of prayer and defense were a success! Hashem decided not to destroy His people immediately. When Moshe heard Hashem calling the Jews "His people" once again, Moshe knew he had succeeded. But they still were not forgiven.

Now that Hashem wasn't going to destroy the Jews right then, Moshe had time to go down and see what he could do about getting them to do teshuvah. Moshe was ready to finish what he had started in heaven — bringing Hashem and the Jews together again.

FASCINATING FACTS

The Jews who worshiped the idol sunk so low that they took the mahn that Hashem sent them from heaven, and brought it to the idol as an offering!

Hashem said He would destroy the Jews and build a new Jewish nation from Moshe alone. But Moshe loved the Jews so much that he refused to become the father of a new Jewish nation. Moshe wouldn't allow the Jews to be destroyed. Instead, he used Hashem's offer as an argument to save the Jews.

Moshe told Hashem, "If You won't forgive the Jewish people even for the sake of their three Avos — Avraham, Yitzchak, and Yaakov — then how will a nation with only one founding father — me — be able to survive if they do wrong? It isn't logical. Right now the Jews are like a chair with three legs, the three Avos. If a three-legged chair can't stand, how can I, just one leg, keep a nation up? It would be a nation supported by only one leg!"

Why didn't Hashem just use smaller print and write out all the commandments on one stone?

Hashem gave it on two stones to teach us that if we keep the Torah we will enjoy two worlds: this world where we live, and also the next world where our souls will be rewarded with tremendous joy.

FASCINATING FACTS

The Luchos were square blocks of sapphire stone, six tefachim tall, six tefachim wide, and three tefachim deep. That's about 2 feet high and wide and a foot thick.

Lifting the Luchos was like carrying two boxes full of rocks. Yet Moshe was able to carry such heavy stone blocks as he walked down a mountain. That he was able to do it was a miracle!

Back to Earth

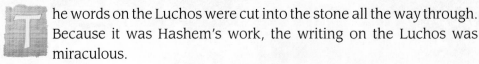

Moshe left heaven with a very precious gift from Hashem: the Luchos.

The Luchos were two square blocks of sapphire stone. Hashem Himself had written the Aseres HaDibros on the stones, five on one stone and five on the other.

Miracle Letters

The words on the Luchos were cut into the stone all the way through. Because it was Hashem's work, the writing on the Luchos was miraculous.

If you carve out the letter samach — ס — on a stone, the middle will fall out. What kept the center piece in place on the Luchos?

You'd have the same problem with the letter "mem sofis," the final "mem" at the end of a word — ם. That is a square. Carve it out, and how does the piece in the center stay up?

But in the Luchos, the center of these two letters just hung in the air without falling out! That was a miracle!

Here's another miracle: The Luchos could be read from both sides. Front and back. When a human cuts words into a stone it's impossible to read the words from the back. The letters in the back would be backward!

Moshe and Yehoshua

The entire time Moshe was away, his devoted student Yehoshua waited at Har Sinai for his rebbi to come back. All alone with no visitors, Yehoshua had no idea what was going on. But he did hear the noise of the Jews celebrating.

When he met Moshe coming down with the Luchos, Yehoshua said, "I hear sounds coming from the Jewish people. I think they are sounds of war." Moshe said, "No, they are not. They are sounds that are making me sad."

Moshe knew the sounds he was hearing were sounds of bad joy. The Jews were enjoying sinning. That made Moshe sad.

Broken!

As they got closer, Moshe saw the Eigel HaZahav and the Jews dancing and singing. He got very angry.

He thought to himself, "How can I give the Torah to people who are acting like non-Jews?"

Miraculously, the letters flew off the stones and went back to heaven. Moshe threw the Luchos down and they shattered into pieces.

Punishments

Moshe's first step to get the Jews to do teshuvah was to punish those people who had actually bowed down to the Eigel HaZahav.

There were different types of these sinners, and they got three types of punishments.

Some people had been warned not to worship the Eigel, and witnesses said they had worshiped the idol anyway. These people were killed by the sword.

Others had not been warned, but witnesses said that they had worshiped the Eigel. These people died in a plague.

Gold Dust

And what about the people who had not been properly warned, and there were no witnesses to say they had worshiped the idol?

Moshe made a large fire and melted the idol down. Then he took the gold metal and ground it down to dust. He sprinkled the gold dust onto a brook that had suddenly started to flow from Har Sinai. He told the Jews to drink from the brook's water.

Those who had worshiped the idol, but hadn't been warned, and there were no witnesses, died when they drank it.

Who Will Kill?

Those who had bowed to the Eigel HaZahav even after being warned by witnesses, were to be killed by the sword.

Who would do it?

Moshe stood in front of the Jews and called out, "Whoever is for Hashem, come join me." One complete shevet, Shevet Levi, answered Moshe's call. They were totally devoted to Hashem and were willing to risk being killed.

They took their swords and killed those who had been warned by witnesses not to sin. They killed 3,000 people, even friends and relatives.

Moshe Moves Away

Because of the sin of the Eigel HaZahav, Moshe moved his tent far away from the place where the Jews were camped. People who wanted to learn from Moshe would go to his tent, outside the camp. Hashem would come to speak with Moshe in his tent, and then Moshe would return to the Jewish camp to teach the Jews what Hashem had said.

Later, when the Mishkan was built, Moshe moved back, and Hashem spoke to him from the Mishkan.

FASCINATING FACTS

Moshe was the greatest prophet. When describing his prophecy, the Torah says that Hashem spoke to Moshe "face to face." This was not said about any other prophet.

___

The job of the firstborn was supposed to be to work in the Mishkan and, later, the Beis HaMikdash. But because they were involved in the sin of the Eigel HaZahav, they lost that privilege. Hashem gave their job to Shevet Levi instead. That was their reward for being the only shevet of which every member stepped forward when Moshe said, "Whoever is for Hashem, come join me."

Moshe Goes Up Again

The next day Moshe told the people, "You have done a great sin. I am going back up to Hashem to beg Him to forgive you."

Moshe went back up Har Sinai for another 40 days.

Erase Me

When Moshe went up to heaven he continued to defend the Jewish people. He said, "It's true the Jews have done a great sin and made a golden idol. But what did You expect? Look at all the gold You gave them."

And then he added, "If You don't forgive them, erase my name from the Torah!" Moshe loved his people so much that if they would be destroyed, he wanted to be destroyed also.

Hashem said, "You shall continue to lead the Jews. I won't destroy them. But in the future, when they have to be punished for a sin, I will add an extra bit of punishment for the sin of the Eigel HaZahav."

To Eretz Yisrael

Hashem said, "The Jews will continue their journey to Eretz Yisrael, the wonderful land that is flowing with milk and honey. But I will not be with them. Instead, I will send an angel who will bring them to Eretz Yisrael and help them conquer the land."

"I don't want that to happen," said Moshe.

Hashem told Moshe, "I will do what you want. Instead of sending an angel, I will go with the Jews."

Moshe asked that Hashem make the Jews special and unique. That His Presence will rest only on the Jews and no other nation.

Hashem agreed.

I Want to See You

Moshe saw that Hashem was being very merciful. His prayers were being answered and Hashem had forgiven the Jews! So he realized it was a good time to ask for even more.

Moshe asked for something for himself. "I want to see Your glory," he said to Hashem.

"You can't see My face," Hashem answered. "No human can see My face and live. But you can stand at the entrance of a cave on Har Sinai. I

FASCINATING FACTS

Because the words of a tzaddik are very powerful, once Moshe said to "erase my name from the Torah," it had to happen. So Hashem "erased" his name — out of just one parashah. In Parashas Tetzaveh, Moshe's name is not mentioned.

QUESTIONS, ANYONE?

What did Hashem let Moshe see?

The knot on the back of His head-tefillin.

On the head-tefillin, the two straps are tied together at the back of the head. Hashem was showing Moshe that He combines a holy thing, like our neshamah, with a physical thing, like our body. This teaches us that we can make the world holy.

will pass by the cave opening, and I will put 'My Palm' on you to protect you until I go by. Then I will remove 'My Palm' and you will be able to see 'My Back.'"

This all sounds very strange. What does this mean? Hashem does not have a body or any shape at all. How can anyone see Hashem? What was Moshe's question and Hashem's answer? Let's look more closely.

Moshe's Question, Hashem's Answer

The Question

Moshe wanted to understand how Hashem runs the world. Why is it that sometimes we see tzaddikim and good people who suffer in this world, and sometimes we see bad people who have a great life? Moshe wanted to be shown the great rewards that are waiting for tzaddikim and good people in the next world.

In this world, Hashem's glory is hidden. If it wasn't, we would never dare disobey Him. Moshe asked to see all of Hashem's glory, so he could understand everything.

The Heavenly Tour

Hashem took Moshe on a tour of all the rooms in heaven. Moshe saw the rewards for Jews who learn Torah, do the mitzvos, and take care of orphans. Then Hashem showed him an enormous room, larger than any of the others, a room filled with great rewards. Moshe asked, "Who gets these rewards?" Hashem answered, "These rewards are for Jews who used their reward while they were alive, so now I give them these rewards for free, because I have forgiven their sins!"

Even someone as great as Moshe could not understand everything that Hashem does. But, as we explained, Hashem did show Moshe some of His glory. Hashem told Moshe that at the top of Har Sinai was a cave. Moshe should stand in it when he came up the mountain to get the Second Luchos.

Hashem said He would pass by and show Moshe as much of His glory as a human being can take without dying. Hashem promised to protect Moshe from the intense power of what he would see. Then Moshe would see and understand some of Hashem's glory.

Hashem also promised that He will teach Moshe how the Jews should pray when they are in trouble and need forgiveness.

A Second Chance

oshe had been up on Har Sinai for forty days, from the 18th of Tammuz to the 29th of Av. During that time he had accomplished a lot. He had begged Hashem to forgive the Jews and Hashem had agreed.

Now the time had come for a second chance. The Jews would once again be given the Luchos with the Aseres HaDibros.

Moshe Becomes Rich

oshe went back to the people after the forty days. Before he went down, Hashem told him to make a new set of stone blocks. He should return to Har Sinai the next morning, and bring the blocks with him. On these blocks Hashem would write the Aseres HaDibros again. Hashem Himself had prepared the stones for the First Luchos. For the Second Luchos, Moshe did it.

Moshe went back to earth and to the Jews. Hashem showed him that at the bottom of his tent he would find sapphire rock. Moshe hammered two blocks of sapphire out of the rock.

Hashem told him to keep the splinters of sapphire that came off the stone as he carved them into squares. They were worth a lot of money, so Moshe was now a rich man.

Up Again

It was the first day of Elul and Moshe went up to get the second set of Luchos. When Moshe first went up to get the Torah, it was in front of all the people, with lightning and thunder and the sound of the shofar.

Not this time! Hashem instructed that this time everything should be done quietly, simply, and modestly. Because when you want something to succeed, it's best to do it quietly.

Hashem Passes By

Moshe stood at the entrance of the cave Hashem had told him about. He anxiously waited for Hashem to pass by.

When the time finally came, Moshe saw a vision of Hashem passing by, wrapped in a tallis. Like we explained, this was an idea, because Hashem has no body or shape. Hashem acted like a chazzan and called out the powerful words that Jews should say when they want forgiveness. These words describe the Thirteen Middos, the traits of Hashem, how He is good, kind, and merciful. (For more on the 13 Middos, see page 174.)

Hashem also gave Moshe a list of things the Jews should be particularly careful about. (To see the list go to page 175.)

Moshe's Mask

Moshe then stayed up in heaven for forty days, learning the Torah from Hashem. During all that time he didn't eat, drink, or sleep. When the forty days were over, Moshe came down with the Second Luchos. It was Yom Kippur.

The Jews watched Moshe coming down. When he came close enough that they could see his face, they began to tremble with fear. They all covered their eyes. They couldn't bear to look at Moshe's face.

What happened? Moshe's face was shining with a great spiritual light. It was so powerful and bright, it wasn't possible for a person to look at his holy face.

This was a gift Hashem had given Moshe. It was a reward for praising the Jews and defending them in the face of Hashem's anger at them.

From then on — except when Moshe taught the Jews Torah or when he spoke to Hashem — he wore a mask to cover the brightness of his face.

FASCINATING FACTS

The 13 Middos in this parashah are read in shul on fast days, when we pray for forgiveness and devote ourselves to teshuvah. They are also said many, many times on Yom Kippur and in Selichos.

A Special Day

The Jews were overjoyed at receiving the Second Luchos. This showed that Hashem had accepted their teshuvah and forgiven them. They were once again on a high level, the Chosen People of Hashem.

Forever after, Yom Kippur became a special day, a day when the Jews would do teshuvah and pray for forgiveness. It became the day when Hashem would forgive the Jews for their mistakes during the year.

The Yeshivah of Moshe Rabbeinu

Now that the Jews had been given the Torah, they were very eager to learn it. Moshe would be their rebbi. Moshe had a very interesting way of teaching in his "yeshivah." He understood the importance of "chazarah," reviewing the Torah a person learned. So Moshe taught in such a way that everyone would learn the same Torah topic four times, just as Hashem had taught it to Moshe four times.

This is how Torah was taught in the "Yeshivah of Moshe Rabbeinu":

Moshe would teach what he learned from Hashem. He would first teach it to Aharon. When he was finished, Aharon stayed in the room, sitting on Moshe's left.

Aharon's sons, Elazar and Issamar, would enter. Moshe would teach the same thing again. Then Elazar and Issamar would split up, Elazar sitting to Moshe's right and Issamar sitting to the left of Aharon.

The Zekeinim, the elder sages of Israel, came in. Moshe repeated his teaching. Afterward the Zekeinim sat on the side. Then all the people entered and Moshe gave the same lesson to the Jewish people. When he was finished teaching them, he left.

Aharon got up and repeated the lesson, and then he left. Then Aharon's sons repeated the lesson and they left.

Finally, the Elders gave the same lesson.

With this system Moshe passed on the entire Torah to the Jewish nation — and each person heard it four times!

TORAH IN OUR LIVES

These forty days, from Rosh Chodesh Elul to Yom Kippur, were days when Hashem was very forgiving of the Jews, even though they had done the terrible sin of the Eigel HaZahav. That's why this became the best time of the year to do teshuvah. It's easier to do teshuvah and gain forgiveness in these forty days than it is during any other time of the year. It's the time that Hashem is ready and waiting for our teshuvah.

The Thirteen Middos of Hashem

These are the 13 middos that we say when we ask Hashem for forgiveness. They describe 13 traits of Hashem.

1. ה' — Hashem: Hashem is merciful before people commit a sin.

2. ה' — Hashem: He is merciful even after people sin. He is ready to forgive them when they are sorry for doing wrong.

3. אֵ-ל — Keil (G-d): His mercy is so strong that no matter how bad a person has behaved, Hashem is ready to forgive!

4. רַחוּם — Rachum (Merciful): He gives light punishment.

5. וְחַנּוּן — V'Chanun (and Gracious): He does good for people who request things from Him, even if they don't deserve it.

6. אֶרֶךְ אַפַּיִם — Erech Apayim (Slow to anger): Hashem waits and waits and waits before punishing someone for what they did wrong. He wants to give people time to do teshuvah.

7. וְרַב חֶסֶד — V'Rav Chessed (and very Kind): If people lack mitzvos, Hashem tips the scale so that the people will be judged as if they had more mitzvos than sins.

8. וֶאֱמֶת — V'Emes (and Truthful): Hashem always gives the rewards He promised for doing good, even to people who otherwise sin.

9. נֹצֵר חֶסֶד לָאֲלָפִים — Notzer Chessed LaAlafim (Keeper of kindness for a thousand generations): The reward for a mitzvah that a person does is also given to children and grandchildren, for two thousand generations.

10. נֹשֵׂא עָוֹן — Nosei Avon (He forgives sin): Hashem forgives people when they do teshuvah, even if they sinned on purpose.

11. וָפֶשַׁע — VaFesha (and forgives serious sin): When people sin not because they want something, but just to make Hashem angry, and they do teshuvah — Hashem will forgive them!

12. וְחַטָּאָה — V'Chata'ah (and forgives sins done by mistake): Hashem forgives people who had sinned because they weren't careful enough, and they now did teshuvah.

13. וְנַקֵּה — V'Nakeh (and Who makes clean): When a person sins and does teshuvah, Hashem cleans the sin off the person's record. He erases it so it's like the sin never happened.

Be Careful!

ashem told Moshe to tell the Jews to be careful with the following mitzvos:

▸ When you go into Eretz Yisrael, don't let the Canaanites remain there. Destroy their idols. Don't make agreements allowing them to stay in the land! If you let them stay, they will cause you to worship idols and your children will intermarry with them.

▸ Don't make idols from melted metal, like you did with the Eigel HaZahav.

▸ Eat matzah on Pesach.

▸ Redeem firstborn baby boys, first-born male bulls, goats, sheep, and donkeys (for more on these mitzvos see Parashas Bo, page 55).

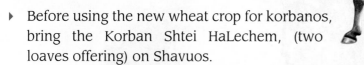

▸ Before using the new wheat crop for korbanos, bring the Korban Shtei HaLechem, (two loaves offering) on Shavuos.

▸ When you come to the Beis HaMikdash on Pesach, Shavuos, and Succos, bring a Korban Olah (burnt offering) on the Mizbei'ach.

▸ On Pesach, Shavuos, and Succos, Jewish men must celebrate the holidays at the Beis HaMikdash.

▸ The Korban Pesach should not be brought if the owner still owns any chametz.

▸ Any part of the Korban Pesach not eaten on Seder night has to be burned on the second day of Pesach.

▸ The Jews must bring Bikkurim. These are the first fruits of a field or orchard to ripen. They are brought to the Beis HaMikdash and given to the Kohanim.

▸ The Torah tells us in three places not to cook a young animal in its mother's milk. This is one of the places. Why is it repeated three times? To teach three things we may not do: We may not cook meat and milk together. We may not eat milk and meat that was cooked together. And we may not have any benefit from the milk and meat mixture.

QUESTIONS, ANYONE?

The Jews all over Eretz Yisrael have a mitzvah to leave their homes three times a year, to come to Yerushalayim to celebrate the holiday and visit the Beis HaMikdash. Who will take care of their homes, their cattle, their fields, to make sure nothing is stolen? What if an enemy decides that the best time to invade is when the Jews are all in Yerushalayim? Who's going to stop them?

Hashem Himself! Not the police and not the army. It was one of the great miracles that happened three times a year as long as the Beis HaMikdash stood. Every Pesach, Shavuos, and Succos, when almost all Jews were in Yerushalayim for Yom Tov, Hashem protected everyone's property. Nothing was stolen and they were never invaded during those times.

פָּרָשַׁת
וַיַּקְהֵל

•

Parashas
Vayakhel

Vayakhel · וַיַּקְהֵל

Parashah Pointers

▸ Moshe speaks to a great assembly of all the Jews. It is the day after he brought down the Second Luchos.

▸ He tells the Jews they should keep Shabbos and build a Mishkan, but they may not build it on Shabbos. It is forbidden to make a fire on Shabbos.

▸ Moshe tells the Jews to go home and bring back whatever they want to donate to build the Mishkan.

▸ The Jews bring so much that very quickly they have everything needed to build the Mishkan — and even more.

▸ Betzalel and Ohaliav are appointed to be in charge of building the Mishkan.

▸ The Jews volunteer to make the different items needed for the Mishkan. Hashem gives extraordinary wisdom and knowledge to everyone involved in building it.

▸ The women also donate their copper mirrors. These mirrors are used to make the Kiyor from which the Kohanim washed their hands and feet before serving in the Mishkan.

▸ All the different parts of the Mishkan are completed.

An Important Announcement

n Yom Kippur, Moshe brought down the Second Luchos. This parashah opens on the day after that great event.

Moshe called all the Jews together — men, women, and children. He announced that Hashem would once again rest His Shechinah on the Jewish people. He had taken it away after the terrible sin of the Eigel HaZahav. This was fantastic news!

Moshe explained that in order for this to happen the Jews would have to build a Mishkan, a place where Hashem's Shechinah would rest.

Then Moshe gave the list of thirteen materials they would need to make the Mishkan and the clothing of the Kohanim. He told the people to go home and bring back whatever they wanted to give. The Jews went home, excited and eager to give their wealth for the Mishkan.

Let's Give

he Jews quickly brought all the materials that were needed. The next day they kept giving, and giving, and giving, until they had more than was needed. Moshe sent out messengers to tell the people, "Stop! Don't bring anything else."

A husband could not donate his wife's jewelry to the Mishkan without her permission.

QUESTIONS, ANYONE?

There is no Mishkan today. So why are we learning about how it was built and what materials were used?

The reward for learning about the Mishkan and working hard to understand how it was built is very great. It helps bring about the rebuilding of the Beis HaMikdash in Yerushalayim.

Who were the first ones to bring donations to the Mishkan?

The women. By the time the men got to the place where the donations were being collected … they found the women were already there!

Moshe made sure to tell the Jews that Hashem Himself had appointed Betzalel to be in charge of the Mishkan. Why?

Moshe didn't want the people to think that he chose Betzalel because they were related. (Betzalel was the great-grandson of Moshe's sister Miriam.) Hashem chose Betzalel because he was the best person for the job.

Holy Women

The women had refused to donate their jewelry for the Eigel HaZahav. But now, when it came to building the Mishkan, the holy Jewish women happily gave away their jewelry in honor of Hashem.

They did not give away only their jewelry. They also gave their mirrors. In those days mirrors were not made of glass, they were made of polished copper metal. All the copper mirrors donated by the women were used to make the Kiyor, the place where the Kohanim washed their hands and feet before working in the Mishkan.

These mirrors were very precious to the Jewish women. In Egypt, they had used these mirrors to make themselves beautiful, which helped keep Jewish families together and led to the growth of the nation.

Only 13!

Sometimes children are much wiser than their age. It's a gift Hashem gives them. Betzalel was such a child. He was only thirteen years old when the Mishkan was built. Hashem had already chosen Betzalel to be in charge of building the Mishkan, from the time when Adam, the first man, was created. Hashem gave Moshe Rabbeinu the plans for the Mishkan and for the clothing of the Kohanim. It was Betzalel's job to see to it that they were made correctly.

Why Betzalel?

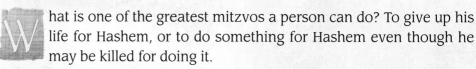

What is one of the greatest mitzvos a person can do? To give up his life for Hashem, or to do something for Hashem even though he may be killed for doing it.

Betzalel's grandfather, Chur, was killed trying to stop the Jews from making the Eigel HaZahav. Chur's mother, Miriam, was one of the Jewish nurses in Egypt. She risked her life when she refused to obey Pharaoh's order to kill the baby boys as soon as they were born.

Betzalel was Chur's grandson and Miriam's great-grandson. As a reward for their brave deeds, Betzalel was put in charge of building the Mishkan.

The Assistant

Betzalel's assistant was Ohaliav, from Shevet Dan. Dan was one of the least honored of the shevatim. Dan wasn't the shevet of Jewish royalty, like Yehudah (which was Betzalel's shevet).

What does Hashem appointing Ohaliav from Dan have to do with us?

Some kids in a class have fathers who are famous Rabbis or roshei yeshivah. Others come from rich families. So what?

All kids should be treated the same and be welcomed to the "chevrah," even if they don't come from famous families or aren't smart and athletic. Didn't Hashem want one of the lowest shevatim to be treated as well as the other shevatim? Didn't He appoint a Danite to such an important position?

You can be a snob, or you can welcome all your classmates with open arms. The choice is up to you. But we know what Hashem wants us to do!

FASCINATING FACTS

There are 39 types of work that we are not allowed to do on Shabbos. Each one is called an "av melachah." They are the types of work that were used to build the Mishkan.

Here's an example. Some of the coverings of the Mishkan were made out of animal hides. To make these coverings, the Jews had to trap animals and kill them. So we are not allowed to trap or kill any living thing on Shabbos.

Dan's mother, Bilhah, wasn't one of Yaakov's main wives, Rachel or Leah. The Danites were also weaker than some of the other shevatim.

Hashem wanted to teach an important lesson, so he appointed a man from Shevet Dan to build the Mishkan together with a man from Shevet Yehudah. This was to show the Jews that in Hashem's eyes all the shevatim are equally important.

Shabbos

At the great assembly when Moshe announced the building of the Mishkan, he first spoke about Shabbos. He told the people that keeping Shabbos is more important than building the Mishkan, so they could not build it on Shabbos.

No Fire

Moshe told the Jews that they shouldn't make a fire to cook and bake on Shabbos. However, we are allowed to cook on Jewish holidays (except for Yom Kippur).

Volunteers

The Jews not only gave their wealth for the Mishkan, but both men and women volunteered to use their skills to make the things needed for it. There were men who worked with gold and silver, carpenters who made beams, and women who wove and sewed curtains for the Mishkan and its roof, and the special clothes for the Kohanim.

Hashem gave everyone special knowledge and skill to be able to create the beautiful Mishkan. For example, he gave women the special knowledge to be able to weave goat hair while it was still on the live animal. That takes special talent.

First Things First

This was the order in which they made the following items for the Mishkan.

1. **Kerashim**: These beams were used to make the walls of the Mishkan building.
2. **Yeri'os:** These coverings would become the roof of the Mishkan.

3. **Paroches:** This curtain hung in front of the Kodesh HaKodashim.

4. **Aron:** The Ark where the Luchos were kept.

5. **Kapores**: The cover on the Aron.

6. **Shulchan:** The Table used to hold the Lechem HaPanim.

7. **Menorah:** Its lamps stayed lit through the night.

8. **Mizbach HaZahav:** The Golden Altar where the Kohanim burned Ketores twice a day.

Again and Again

any of the verses in the parashah discuss the construction of the Mishkan and the items inside it. Often, the verses seem to repeat what we were taught in Parashas Terumah.

This was done to teach us how very precious the Mishkan was to Hashem.

FASCINATING FACTS

Not only did Hashem give the Jews wisdom and knowledge, but He even gave them the animal they needed for the Mishkan. The tachash animal came on its own to Moshe.

Rome

Whatever happened to the Paroches that hung in the Second Beis HaMikdash?

It was taken to Rome.

How do we know?

Once, in the time of the Gemara, the Romans made laws forbidding the Jews to keep Shabbos and bris milah. R' Shimon bar Yochai and R' Elazar bar R' Yose went to Rome to convince the Romans to cancel the evil decrees. When they got there the Caesar's daughter was very sick, and R' Shimon miraculously healed her. As a reward, the Caesar allowed the Rabbis to enter the treasure rooms of Rome and take whatever they wanted.

The Rabbis weren't interested in gold or silver or money! They searched for the scrolls on which the Romans wrote the evil laws. When they found the scrolls, they ripped them up. Now the Jews could keep Shabbos and bris milah without breaking the law.

R' Elazar later told the Rabbis that while they were there he saw the Paroches. The Romans had taken it to Rome when they destroyed the Beis HaMikdash. It still had the bloodstains of the Yom Kippur korbanos that had been offered before the Beis HaMikdash was destroyed.

פָּרָשַׁת פְּקוּדֵי

◆

Parashas Pekudei

Pekudei · פְּקוּדֵי

Parashah Pointers

▸ Moshe shows the Jews how their donations for the Mishkan were used.

▸ The Mishkan and the clothing for the Kohanim are all completed and brought to Moshe by the 25th of Kislev.

▸ Miraculously, Moshe puts up the Mishkan all by himself on the 23rd of Adar.

▸ From the 23rd of Adar until Rosh Chodesh Nissan, Moshe serves as a Kohen Gadol and performs the services in the Mishkan, while spiritually preparing the Mishkan and showing Aharon and his sons what to do.

▸ Rosh Chodesh Nissan is a day of celebration, the first day the Mishkan is permanently open. On that day the Shechinah comes to rest on the building that the Jewish people had made — the Mishkan. This shows the Jews that Hashem accepted their teshuvah for the sin of the Eigel HaZahav.

Let's Count

Moshe called all the Jews together. In front of everyone, he gave an exact count of what they had donated for the Mishkan. Moshe let them know how all the money and materials had been used. He did this so no one should suspect that he had taken any of the donations for himself.

Moshe knew that he hadn't taken anything. Hashem knew Moshe hadn't taken anything. The people trusted Moshe. So why did he make a big public event to show that he hadn't taken anything?

Moshe was teaching us to be very careful with tzedakah (charity) money. We must make sure that the money was used the right way or that someone was not stealing money. For example, someone who was just put in charge of a shul's tzedakah fund shouldn't suddenly start wearing expensive new clothes. Even though the person bought it with his own money, we have to make sure that no one would even suspect that he took the shul's money to pay for it. A person should do what is right in the eyes of Hashem — and in the eyes of people!

The Mystery of the Missing Silver

Moshe reported, "The people gave 301,775 shekels of silver. Three hundred thousand shekels of silver were used to make the Adanim, the silver bases, of the Mishkan walls. The rest, 1,775 silver shekels, were used for…" Then Moshe stopped. He couldn't remember what that silver had been used for! Moshe was afraid the Jews would think he stole it!

There was silence. Everyone was waiting for Moshe to announce what had been done with the 1,775 shekels of silver. Moshe was silent. It seemed he didn't know. Suddenly the silence was broken by a loud Heavenly voice. It said:

"1,775 silver shekels were used for the silver hooks on the pillars."

Now everyone knew — and Moshe's honor was saved.

In the time of the Second Beis HaMikdash, Kohanim from the family of Avtinas made the sweet-smelling Ketores. Their wives and daughters did not use perfume, so that no one would think they took some of the Ketores home for themselves.

The Beis HaMikdash had a room where they kept the money that people gave. A person who went into that room wore clothes with no pockets or cuffs, so no one could think he was taking money for himself.

The word "Mishkan" is repeated twice in the first verse of the parashah. Why is that?

The Mishkan — and later the Beis HaMikdash — was a place for Jews to serve Hashem here on earth. There is also a Beis HaMikdash in Heaven! That's why it says "Mishkan" twice.

The Jews had brought more than was needed to make the Mishkan. After the Mishkan was completed Moshe saw how much was left over. He didn't know what to do with the extra materials.

So he asked Hashem. Hashem told him to use the extra materials to build a large tent, where the Jews would gather to learn Torah and decide Jewish law. In other words — to build a yeshivah!

———

Once the Mishkan was put up, one of the jobs of the Levi'im was to take it apart when the Jews traveled. They would carry all the pieces to the new place the Jews were going to, and then put the Mishkan together.

If you have ever moved you know what a big job it is. Someone had to organize all the Levi'im involved in the move. He had to make sure that everyone knew exactly what his job was. He had to decide who would take the Mishkan apart, who would carry which pieces, and who would put it all together. Without the right man in charge, a piece of the Mishkan could get broken, lost, or left behind!

Moshe appointed Aharon's son Issamar to be in charge of organizing all the Levi'im to move the Mishkan.

Issamar and the Levi'im did a very good job. The Jews moved many times in the desert, yet nothing from the Mishkan was ever lost or broken!

Thin, Very Thin

The Torah tells us how the Jews made the clothing for the Kohanim, which was described in Parashas Tetzaveh.

Some of the Kohen Gadol's clothing contained gold thread. How was this thread made? A piece of gold was pounded with a hammer until it was paper thin. Then the gold was cut into thin strips with a knife, creating gold thread.

Done!

The making of all the parts of the Mishkan was finished by the 25th day of Kislev — which more than a thousand years later would become the first day of Chanukah. That means it took about two and a half months to make all the parts.

When everything was done, the Jews brought all the pieces to Moshe. They were all looking forward to putting all the parts together to build the Mishkan. Everyone was proud of their work, and they wanted to see what the Mishkan would look like when it was put up.

Most important of all, they wanted the Shechinah of Hashem to rest on their Mishkan. That would be the sign that Hashem had forgiven them for the sin of the Eigel HaZahav.

It Didn't Happen

The Jews were disappointed when things didn't turn out as they expected.

Moshe was so happy to see that the Jews had made everything as Hashem had wanted that he blessed them that Hashem's Presence should rest on their fine work. But then Moshe told them to put everything into storage. The Mishkan wouldn't be opened for use until Rosh Chodesh Nissan, three months later! The Jews were disappointed but accepted Hashem's plans.

The Connection

Why did Hashem want the Mishkan's first day to be in Nissan? Because that was the month when Yitzchak Avinu was born.

How are Yitzchak and the Mishkan connected?

Yitzchak was willing to give up his life for Hashem at the Akeidah. As a reward for his loyalty to Hashem, Yitzchak's children — and that includes us! — are forgiven when they need forgiveness. It is also through the service and prayers in the Mishkan that Hashem forgives the Jews.

By opening the Mishkan in the month when Yitzchak was born, Hashem connected the forgiveness we get because of Yitzchak with the forgiveness we get because of the Mishkan.

Seven Days of Preparation

Finally, on the 23rd day of Adar, a week before Rosh Chodesh Nissan, the Jews were told to put together the Mishkan. In order for it to open on Rosh Chodesh Nissan, Aharon and his sons would first need seven days of preparation. During that week the Mishkan would be prepared spiritually.

Hanging in the Air

Moshe went to the large, heavy curtain that would cover the Mishkan. The walls were not put up yet. He lifted the curtain and spread it out in the air, where it stayed.

The people could not believe their eyes! The curtain just stayed there, hanging in the air! It didn't fall back to earth!

That was the first miracle on that day. There were more to come.

Moshe held the beams with his holy hands. No strain, no huffing and puffing. The heavy beams just rose up. They stood up on the ground under the curtain that was hanging in the air. The beams stayed until they were in place and fitted together to make the Mishkan walls, with the roof curtain laying on top of them.

Piece by piece, Moshe Rabbeinu put the entire Mishkan together, all by himself! He moved all the large, heavy pieces, like the Aron, the solid gold Menorah, the Golden Mizbei'ach, and the Shulchan into place.

Final Touch

Everything was put together, but there was one last thing to be done.

What was left to do?

The final touch. Moshe took the Shemen HaMishchah and smeared a small amount of oil on each and every part of the Mishkan. Then, after dressing Aharon and his sons in the special clothing of Kohanim, Moshe poured some oil on them as well.

FASCINATING FACTS

Really, the honor of being the day that the Mishkan opened should have gone to the 25th day of Kislev. Many years later, Hashem gave a special honor to that day. There would be a time when the Syrian-Greeks would make the Beis HaMikdash into a Temple for avodah zarah (idols). The Maccabees finally defeated the Syrian-Greeks on the 25th day of Kislev — which is the first day of Chanukah!

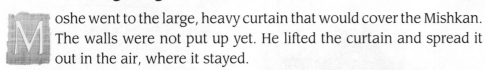

A Kohen for Seven Days

very day, for the next seven days, Moshe put the Mishkan up and then took it down. By himself! During those days, he was a Kohen Gadol. He performed all the Mishkan services and prepared Aharon and his sons to become the Kohanim. He taught them what they needed to know to work in the Mishkan.

The Order of Putting the Mishkan Together

This is how the Torah describes how the Mishkan was put up:

First: The walls and roof of the Mishkan building were put together.

Second: The Luchos containing the Aseres HaDibros were placed in the Aron, and the poles were put into the rings on the sides of the Aron.

Third: The Kapores was placed on the Aron.

Fourth: The Aron was moved into its location at the back of the Heichal. Then the curtain was hung up in front of it.

Fifth: The Shulchan was moved in.

Sixth: The Menorah was brought in.

Seventh: The Golden Mizbei'ach was brought in.

Eighth: The cover to the Heichal entrance was hung up.

Ninth: The Copper Mizbei'ach was set up outside the Heichal entrance.

Tenth: The Kiyor was placed next to the Copper Mizbei'ach and filled with water.

Eleventh: The beams, curtains, and entrance curtain of the Chatzer were put up.

Mazel Tov!

he big day finally came. On Rosh Chodesh Nissan the Mishkan was put up, and this time it was not taken apart. The entire Jewish people gathered around the Mishkan and watched as Hashem's Presence came to rest on the Mishkan. Hashem had forgiven them for the sin of the Eigel HaZahav!

It was a day of great joy and celebration for the nation of Israel.

Chazak Chazak V'nischazeik

We have reached the end of the second of the Five Books of the Torah — Sefer Shemos.

Sefer Shemos opens with one Jewish family. Yaakov Avinu, his children, and grandchildren are now living in Egypt. There they are forced to become the lowest of the low in Egyptian society — slaves.

Sefer Shemos closes with the family that went down to Egypt becoming a great nation, the greatest on earth, chosen by Hashem to be His. The nation He loves. The nation upon whom He rests His Shechinah, in the Mishkan that they built for Him. This is Klal Yisrael, the nation that has a mission: to teach the world that Hashem created the world, still cares about the world, and runs the world.

This is a nation committed to the holy mission they received at Sinai: to listen to Hashem's will, to do the mitzvos, to learn and keep the Torah.

Today, more than 3,300 years after the things that Sefer Shemos tells us about, we are still Hashem's most beloved nation, committed to His Torah!

Glossary

Akeidas Yitzchak: When Avraham Avinu brought his son Yitzchak to be a korban

Am segulah: Treasured nation (the Jews)

Ananei HaKavod: Clouds of Glory (that surrounded the Jews and protected them in the desert)

Aron: The box where the Ten Commandments were kept, located in the Holy of Holies

Aseres HaDibros: Ten Commandments

Avinu: Our father

Bechor: Firstborn

Bedikas Chametz: Search for chametz the night before Pesach

Beis Din: Jewish court

Beis HaMikdash: The holy Temple in Yerushalayim

Beis midrash: Study hall, place where Torah is learned by a group

Berachah (berachos): Blessing(s)

Bris milah: Circumcision

Chametz: Flour and water mixed together and left for over 18 minutes. Chametz is not allowed on Passover.

Chatzer: Mishkan Courtyard

Chessed: Kindness

Chillul Hashem: Desecration of Hashem's Name

Emunah: Faith

Eretz Yisrael: Land of Israel

Erev Pesach: The day before Pesach

Halachah: Jewish law

Hallel: A prayer of praise, said on certain occasions including holidays and Rosh Chodesh

Heichal: Mishkan building

Keruvim: Cherubim, statues in the shape of angels that were on the Aron

Ketores: Sweet-smelling incense burned daily on the Golden Mizbei'ach.

Kohen (Kohanim): Children of Aharon who serve Hashem in special ways

Korban: Offering brought in the Mishkan or Beis HaMikdash

Lashon hara: Speaking badly about someone, which is not allowed by Jewish law.

Luchos: Two tablets that contained the Ten Commandments

Mahn: Manna, miraculous food the Jews ate in the desert

Makkah (Makkos): Plague(s)

Maror: A very bitter herb

Mashiach: The Messiah, a descendant of King David. We are all waiting for him to come.

Mattan Torah: Giving of the Torah

Mishkan: Tabernacle, place where Hashem rested His Presence

Mitzrayim: Egypt

Mitzvah (mitzvos): Commandment(s)

Mizbei'ach: Altar

Nasi (Nesi'im): Prince(s) of a tribe

Parashah: Portion of the Torah

Rosh Chodesh: The beginning of a new Jewish month. Sometimes it also includes the last day of the previous month.

Sanhedrin: Highest Jewish court

Shacharis: Morning prayers

Shamayim: Heaven

Shechinah: Hashem's Presence

Shechitah: The way to slaughter an animal that is according to halachah

Shevet (shevatim): Tribe(s)

Shul: Synagogue

Siyum: Celebration marking the completion of a part of the Torah or Talmud

Tahor: Pure

Tamei: Not pure

Teivah: The boat that saved Noach and his family

Teshuvah: Repentance

Tzaddik: A pious and good man

Yetzer hara: Something inside that tempts a person to do wrong

Yetzias Mitzrayim: The exodus from Egypt

Yom Tov: Holiday

Yovel: Jubilee, 50th year in the Shemittah cycle

Sources

MRS = Midrash Rabbah Shemos
MT = Midrash Tanchuma
MTS = Midrash Tanchuma Shemos
YSS = Yalkut Shimoni Shemos

Parashas Yisro